Vintage dresses, timeless stories

Dreaming of Chanel

Charlotte Smith

Illustrated by Grant Cowan

ATRIA BOOKS

New York London Toronto Sydney New Delhi

ATRIA BOOKS
A Division of Simon & Schuster, Inc.
1230 Avenue of the Americas
New York, NY 10020

Text copyright © 2010 by Charlotte Smith
Images copyright © 2010 by Grant Cowan

Originally published in English in Sydney, Australia, in 2010 by HarperCollins*Publishers* Australia, Pty Limited.

This North American edition is published by arrangement with HarperCollins*Publishers* Australia, Pty Limited.

First Atria Books hardcover edition November 2011

ATRIA BOOKS and colophon are registered trademarks of Simon & Schuster, Inc.

For information about special discounts for bulk purchases, please contact Simon & Schuster Special Sales at 1-866-506-1949 or business@simonandschuster.com.

The Simon & Schuster Speakers Bureau can bring authors to your live event. For more information or to book an event, contact the Simon & Schuster Speakers Bureau at 1-866-248-3049 or visit our website at www.simonspeakers.com.

Designed by Jay Ryves at Future Classic, adapted by Jane Waterhouse, HarperCollins Design Studio

Manufactured in China

10 9 8 7 6 5 4 3 2 1

Library of Congress Cataloging-in-Publication Data

Smith, Charlotte M.
   Dreaming of Chanel : vintage dresses, timeless stories / Charlotte Smith ; illustrated by Grant Cowan.—1st Atria books hardcover ed.
       p.   cm.
   "Originally published in English in Sydney, Australia, in 2010 by HarperCollinsPublishers Australia" Companion to Dreaming of Dior.
   1. Darnell, Doris Hastings, 1916– 2007—Art collections.   2. Women's clothing—Private collections.   3. Women's clothing—History.   4. Vintage clothing—Private collections.   I. Cowan, Grant.   II. Smith, Charlotte M. Dreaming of Dior.   III. Title.
   GT1720.S613 2011
   391'.2—dc22   2011007939

ISBN 978-1-4516-3295-8
ISBN 978-1-4516-3298-9 (ebook)

For Howard and Olivia

I have to confess that when my American godmother Doris Darnell told me her priceless vintage clothing collection was on its way across the world to me, I was more than a little daunted. Doris's collection had been a lifetime labour of love for her, more precious than any treasure I knew of, and she had chosen me as custodian.

Never in my wildest dreams could I have predicted how much this precious legacy would change my life, mind lead me to writing my first book, *Dreaming of Dior*.

It all began when I opened the first box at my home in the Blue Mountains to find an exquisite gossamer silk 1920s evening gown shimmering with the most intricately beautiful beadwork I had ever seen. I had unearthed my first treasure. I was instantly enchanted, as Doris knew I would be.

Doris was the ultimate fairy godmother. When I was growing up near Philadelphia in Pennsylvania, I was a regular visitor at Doris and Howard's townhouse. As soon as I arrived Doris and I would climb the impossibly narrow and steep staircase to the top floor and lose ourselves for an hour or two amid her latest acquisitions and old favourites. For me this was where magic happened, brought alive by Doris's wonderful stories about the dresses and the women who wore them.

Spanning two hundred and five years, from 1790 to 1995, her collection is a journey through fashion history encompassing famous couturiers like Dior, Chanel and Vionnet. But not one piece was purchased by her. They are all gifts from friends and acquaintances who either knew or had heard of her legendary 'hobby'. As the Quaker saying goes, every piece was 'given in love and in trust'. Doris was a Quaker her whole life, and while her passion for clothes and accessories was frowned upon as immodest and frivolous by other practising Quakers, her passion remained as irrepressible as her character.

Doris devoted the last few decades of her life to sharing her collection with the world. Throughout the 1970s and 1980s, Doris became well known throughout the East Coast of the United States and beyond for her 'living fashion' talks, which she would give in museums, college halls and even on cruises around the world, including the *QEII*, donating her speaking fees to the Quaker Society of Friends.

Doris's audiences were invariably so enchanted by her shows that they would donate some of their own treasures to the collection. And so the collection continued to grow, more and more stories were added to share, until the baton was passed on to me.

The treasures that lay before me were worth a fortune. Selling them would set me up for life, but enticing as that thought was, I could never consider such a thing or the idea of them being broken up by donation to museums or other collections. I still had no idea what to do with the collection, but somehow, like Doris, I would find a way to share it and to keep it growing.

Then, among the last of Doris's boxes, I found her catalogue notes of all her stories, of the dresses and the women who wore them. It was then that the true value of what I had been bequeathed hit home. This wasn't a mere collection of beautiful things, it was a collection of life. Women's lives. Tiny snapshots of our joys and disappointments, our entrances and exits, triumphant and tragic.

This is how my first book, *Dreaming of Dior*, was born. It was the perfect way to share these stories, including Doris's and mine, along with the collection.

The response to my book was beyond my wildest dreams. Strangers came up to me at events or wrote to me, telling how much they loved the stories and the memories they brought back of their own wonderful moments. My only regret is that Doris is no longer here to share the applause.

But the greatest gift from the collection is my new friendship with Doris's husband, Howard. I will always treasure the lovely handwritten letter he sent me after receiving his copy of *Dreaming of Dior*: 'What a fantastic surprise you have given me. The book is spectacular, and for me it is the personal gift of a lifetime.'

I was also delighted and relieved to hear from Doris's son, Eric, and her granddaughter, Fran, that Doris would be so proud and happy with what I have done for her collection. Also to hear from the daughters of Doris's friends that they are thrilled their mother's dresses and stories are included in the book. And, after a twenty-year lull, my father, Noble, now regularly writes Howard and keeps him abreast of what I'm up to.

Most of all, the collection has brought me even closer to Doris. She may no longer be here but I feel she is looking down on all this and thoroughly enjoying the ride with me. And so, in the spirit of love and trust, I - and the inimitable Doris Darnell - open our wardrobe again and share some more unforgettable moments with you now.

Charlotte Smith

P.S. Those of you who have already shared part of the journey with me in *Dreaming of Dior* will have read the following letter Doris wrote, bequeathing her collection to me. But I have included it again for those who are coming to our story - and stories - for the first time. After all, I often reread it to remind myself of just how lucky I am to have such a wonderful fairy godmother.

Dearest Charlotte,

You cannot imagine how happy I am to learn that you are thrilled to have me pass on to you my collection of clothing and accessories of other eras.

Ever since I was a teenager, I have loved to dress up and I still do! Family and friends and friends of friends heard of the old trunk in my attic where I stored my dress-up clothes and started adding to my collection as they cleared out ancestral attics and wondered what to do with all that stuff. That's when my collection really started to grow!

It's been hard, if not impossible, for me to turn down any gifts, because I soon discovered that I was not just collecting dress-up clothes, but, in addition, each piece was a springboard to history. Each donor told me the story of the woman or man who wore the clothing, fascinating stories of other times, sometimes full of joy, other times grief, sometimes bitterness, other times heartache. In my opinion these stories make my clothing three dimensional and in some odd way the people who wore the clothing come alive again in the telling. I am giving you all the stories so that they can continue to be an extension of each outfit.

You ask me what everything I am giving you is worth if you have to declare a value. I have a hard time with that question. I have never bought a single thing nor has anything been appraised. I am giving you a part of my life. I have been a trusted custodian and I am delighted that you see yourself in that same capacity.

The contents of our home are insured for a modest amount with no mention of my clothing. If our house burned down and we lost everything, all of the stories, the glimpses of history, would have no value without the clothing. Money could not replace what I had lost, so why insure?

If I had to come up with something, I would call my gift to you 'old-fashioned clothing with stories about the people who wore the clothes'. They have been treasured by me, but never evaluated. I had planned to leave everything to you in my will, dear godchild, but I am 87 years of age and feel now is the time. So here it is with my blessing!

Love, love, Doris

Inheriting a priceless vintage clothing collection from my American godmother Doris Darnell was unexpected, exciting and downright scary. I was honoured but more than a little daunted at the prospect of becoming custodian of what had been a lifetime's labour of love.

Once Doris broke the news to me, I had eight months to consider how I was going to live up to the challenge while the collection made its way here from the other side of the world - all 3500 pieces and 1200 kilos of it.

But the day I pulled back the packing tape on the first box and gingerly lifted out the first dress from its layers of protective white tissue, all my fears flew away.

Gossamer cream silk, covered in glittering silver and white glass beads, slipped through my fingers as I held it up to the light. It was a 1920s evening dress - exquisite. I was enchanted, as Doris knew I would be.

And I knew this collection was going to change my life.

All my life I have dreamed of owning the ultimate couture piece, a Chanel suit. Inheriting the collection spurred me to make that dream a reality. While a new Chanel suit was way out of my league, vintage was another story.

I found my dream online in America - a classic dusty pink Chanel wool skirt suit from the 1960s, with signature braid trim and filigree buttons.

Now I just had to fight for it at auction - at three o'clock in the morning! Determined to leave nothing to chance, I set four alarm clocks and arranged with the auctioneer to call me the minute my suit came up.

Suddenly the phone rings, and we're off at a cracking pace. My heart pounds as I join the frenzy of bidding and then an eternity seems to pass before the hammer bangs down and the auctioneer exclaims: 'Sold to Miss Down Under!'

At last - my very own Chanel. And at that moment I felt like I had earned every precious thread of it.

As a footnote, after celebrating a very special birthday with my family in America, I now also have the ultimate accessory to go with my suit - a genuine Chanel brooch!

Blanche Wonderly was one of only a handful of women to gain a medical degree at the turn of the century. Sadly Blanche's mother didn't live to see her daughter achieve her dream. She died while Blanche was still studying to become a doctor, leaving her husband and daughter heartbroken.

As was the custom in those days, Blanche's father suggested that his daughter should buy a formal black mourning gown. Having never owned a formal dress, Blanche decided that in her mother's memory she would ensure it was the finest and most elegant imaginable.

Blanche's black net gown was certainly that, costing her father the princely sum of $90, a small fortune in 1904. The day Blanche finally qualified to become a doctor, her father took her aside and asked her to give up her dream of practising medicine to take care of him instead.

Like any dutiful daughter of that era, Blanche felt she must obey her father's wishes, and spent the rest of her life caring for him and running his household. She never married and never practised medicine.

Aunt Blanche, as she was lovingly known to everyone, was generous to a fault but she never gave away her $90 dress.

An invitation from a dashing Englishman to stay at the Monte Carlo Beach Hotel for the weekend called for some serious 1980s glamour. This sensational blue swimsuit and matching wrap was just the thing to make me feel the part alongside all the jetsetters at play in the South of France.

While my host had quite a reputation as a ladies' man, if you were his woman of the moment you were in for a truly romantic time and assured of being thoroughly spoiled. So my room was the last word in luxury, tucked away in a private enclave of suites surrounding a large pool, lined by immaculate yellow and white striped deck chairs and terracotta pots overflowing with red geraniums.

On Saturday a gleaming chrome and white motor launch was waiting at the hotel's private jetty, next door to Chanel designer Karl Lagerfeld's chateau, to take us to lunch at one of the Riviera's most famous restaurants, Carpaccio, at Villefranche-sur-Mer. Waiters attended to our every need as we enjoyed platters of lobster and chilled chablis - and a view to die for.

Years later I heard that my date married the daughter of a billionaire. And I remembered that day when he made me feel like a million dollars.

When Ellen Brown was invited to a fabulous party in the late 1940s, her excitement gave way to despair when she realised she couldn't afford a new dress.

But Ellen was a determined and resourceful young lady and a little financial crisis wasn't going to stop her. Inspiration struck when she remembered that her parents had luckily held on to the blush pink velvet curtains that used to hang in her grandmother's living room.

So, like Scarlett in *Gone with the Wind*, Ellen showed just what a creative woman can do at a pinch. She rolled up her sleeves and transformed the curtains into a show-stopping party frock - with her own twist on Dior's classic 'New Look' fitted bodice and full skirt that was all the rage - and sailed into the party looking like she had just walked off the runway.

No one would ever have guessed that this glamorous model of elegance was wearing her grandmother's curtains. No doubt every woman in the room would have been enviously wondering where she could buy one just like it.

In Edwardian times, wearing all white was not only considered the height of fashion but a reflection of a lady's wealth and social standing.

Socialite Edith Rodman boasted an entire wardrobe of what became known as Edwardian Whites, all exquisitely handmade and embroidered.

As the wife of a prominent businessman from Pittsburgh, Edith was kept busy with a constant round of social engagements, from afternoon tea parties and tennis matches to evening soirees. She had more than a dozen white gowns made for her in the best quality linen or lawn, all featuring the finest embroidery money could buy.

Her favourite was this day dress with dramatic cutwork on the skirt, a masterpiece that took one seamstress more than six months to create.

Stepping out in this dress, with a matching parasol and spectacular ostrich feather hat, she would have fit right in alongside Audrey Hepburn in the famous Royal Ascot scene in *My Fair Lady*.

All my friends know how passionate I am about my collection so they keep an eye out for treasures for me.

When my friend Adrian Franklin caught sight of this divine 1960s daffodil yellow silk dress in the window of one of Hobart's best vintage shops, Collectibles, he had to investigate. When he saw the label 'Mona Crawford, Sydney' he knew I'd have to have it as I'm always on the lookout for more Australian designers to add to my collection.

Featuring an intricate overlay of lace daisies, it was a bargain at $25, especially when Adrian discovered Mona Crawford had created another distinctive silk and lace dress featuring a wreath of native flowers for Miss Australia, Tania Verstak, to wear at the Miss International contest in California in 1962.

Beyond her winning poise and beauty, Tania is remembered as the first migrant or then 'new Australian' to be crowned Miss Australia, and fittingly she broke years of stuffy tradition by wearing her Mona Crawford dress - the previous contestant had worn a British riding outfit. Best of all, Tania went on to win the title of Miss International.

Which makes this a genuine Australian treasure.

When I was working for Acquavella Galleries in New York in the 1980s, the son of an international art collector invited me out for drinks.

I met my date at his parents' apartment, which happened to be in the swanky Carlisle Hotel building on Madison Avenue, where we didn't have to go far for our drinks - we just popped downstairs to the bar.

Chilled Bellinis in long-stemmed crystal flutes magically appeared and just when I thought things couldn't be better, I discovered that the legendary Bobby Short was playing the piano that night.

So we settled into a dark and romantic corner of the bar while Bobby bewitched us all with the best of everything from Cole Porter and Gershwin to Duke Ellington.

Wearing this black wool number with glittering bead trim, I felt a little like the torch singer Michelle Pfeiffer played in *The Fabulous Baker Boys*. But I was more than happy to just look good and listen - and enjoy the magic of a master at work.

By the early 1950s Christian Dior's elegant wasp-waisted 'New Look' had taken the world by storm and the little country town of Canowindra in New South Wales was no exception.

Canowindra may not have had any designer boutiques but they were hardly necessary when one of their own could create stunning creations like this.

After joining the weekly sewing circle at the church hall, young Barbara Coty proved to be so gifted that she won a scholarship to East Sydney Technology College. It was the boom years when Australia was 'riding on the sheep's back' and her father could afford to indulge his daughter. So whenever Barbara needed fabric for her latest creation she would stroll down to Morlands Silks in the St James building and put whatever she wanted on her father's account.

Barbara hand-painted the polka dots on this gloriously frothy silk confection she made to wear to her graduation ball in 1951. Cinched in at the waist into a dramatically full skirt, it's the epitome of Dior's divine La Corolle silhouette, inspired by the petals of a flower.

Some women live to entertain. And because they entertain so often they need not just one, but several wardrobes full of evening dresses.

Marjorie Mosteller was one of these women. Married to a wealthy industrialist who moved in many different circles, she regularly threw dinners and parties to entertain politicians, movie stars and socialites.

With all these parties to mastermind, Marjorie had a trick to save time with her clothes shopping and avoid being seen in the same dress twice.

Each season she would go to Saks Fifth Avenue in New York and spend the day trying on dresses by her favourite designers. Once she had decided on the style, she would order the dress in every colour it came in.

Once she'd fallen for this heavenly floaty silk chiffon dress by American designer Bill Blass, she ordered it in lime green, hot pink, sapphire blue, navy, cream, red and black.

Presto - one week's worth of parties sorted.

In the 1960s the 'youthquake' movement in fashion and music in London was reverberating around the world. Coined by *Vogue's* editor-in-chief Diana Vreeland, the fun, spirited and youthful look was epitomised by designers like Mary Quant. Poster girls included models like Twiggy, Jean Shrimpton, Penelope Tree and Veruschka.

Those with a little more cash to splash embraced the bold and wildly colourful prints of Italian designer Emilio Pucci, who first caught the attention of the fashion world for designing skiwear, of all things. After a *Harper's Bazaar* photographer snapped a friend wearing one of his sleek creations, Pucci was asked to design skiwear for a 1948 issue of *Harper's*, and the rest is history.

Pucci's haute couture headquarters on the Isle of Capri helped establish him as a darling of the international jetset. Tanned, beautiful people flocked there or to his boutique in Rome to buy their own piece of the distinctive prints worn by everyone from Marilyn Monroe and Sophia Loren to Jackie Kennedy.

Today a whole new generation is discovering that a sensational Pucci print skirt like this, ideally with matching accessories, spells instant glamour.

W hen my godmother Doris was not adding to her collection, she was enjoying her working life as a librarian at Westtown, a Quaker school in Pennsylvania's Chester County. Founded in 1799, the school espouses the Friends' values: simplicity, peace, integrity, community and equality.

Typically, Doris would be the first to notice anyone who looked a little left out and bring them in to her fold, an ideal quality for her later role as Personnel Director of the American Friends Service Committee. When she saw a new faculty wife looking lost and lonely one cold October day, Doris stopped to chat and promptly invited her home for tea.

It was the beginning of a beautiful friendship and an annual tradition. As they chatted and discovered they shared a love of music, sailing, travel and many other things, her new friend Pat confessed that it also happened to be her birthday.

Delighted, Doris insisted they have an impromptu celebration. From then on the two friends made a fine habit of celebrating that day together every year.

As Pat had been wearing her favourite long 1950s red coat that first October day, she always wore it when she and Doris celebrated 'their' birthday.

Trawling through the treasures in my mother's writing desk one day, my daughter Olivia discovered a grand gold-deckled invitation tucked between two black and white photographs. It read: *The Lord Chamberlain is commanded by Their Majesties to summon Miss Margaret Stafford to an afternoon presentation tea party at Buckingham Palace on Tuesday the 13th of March, 1951.*

The photographs showed my mother dressed in an elegant silver and black striped dress, with a fashionably full skirt cinched in tightly at the waist by a black belt, a demure black saucer hat, matching pumps, gloves and clutch. She looked so sophisticated and yet so very young.

The honour of being presented at court followed tradition in my mother's family. Her mother, my grandmother, May Bevan Stafford, had been presented to King George V and Queen Mary in 1914. My grandmother was granted the privilege in turn of arranging for the presentation of her daughter, daughter-in-law and niece.

While my grandmother's presentation in 1914 would have been a very formal affair, after the war the event became the more casual and inclusive garden party my mother was invited to. But for Olivia, the mere idea of her grandmother meeting kings and queens was magic.

Jimmy'z nightclub in Monte Carlo was the only place to be if you were young and out on the town in the 1990s. All the beautiful people - impossibly gorgeous blondes and dark and dangerously handsome men - were curled up together in the candle-lit suede booths, reminding me of Somerset Maugham's infamous quote that Monte Carlo was 'a sunny place for shady people'.

One side of the club opened out onto a spectacular ocean view, the perfect vantage point to admire the elegant lines of all the luxury yachts bobbing in the harbour, but anybody who was somebody was seated in the booths closest to the dance floor. As our group included a prince, we were led straight there and waited on hand and foot.

Thanks to our royal friend, as soon as we ventured out onto the dance floor, the great wall of bopping bodies parted so we had all the space we needed to shimmy to Madonna's 'Material Girl'. In my slinky gold metallic dress and plenty of bling, I think I did a fine impersonation.

Kate Ludwig was a highly sought-after professional dressmaker who worked from her home in a well-heeled enclave of Boalsburg, Pennsylvania, in the early 1900s. Every lady in town knew that if she wanted a dream wedding dress and trousseau that would be the envy of all her friends, she needed to call on 'Miss Ludwig'.

When it was finally Kate's turn, for the year leading up to her wedding in 1911, she spent every spare moment handstitching and embroidering her wedding dress and a trousseau full of gowns for day and evening, capes, petticoats and delicate and flirty peignoirs like this.

Peignoirs were an absolute must for ladies of the day. Named from the French word *peigner*, meaning to comb the hair, these long outer wraps certainly began life in a lady's boudoir. Usually made from very fine or almost sheer material, peignoirs were worn over a petticoat and chemise in the mornings.

When a lady sat down wearing a peignoir, it should fall open at just the right point to reveal the full glory of her lace petticoat from the waist down.

Tragically, Kate never had the opportunity to show hers off because the day before her wedding her fiancé jilted her, announcing that he had fallen in love with someone else.

The first time Doris's mother-in-law Helen wore this snazzy bathing suit in 1910 she didn't go near water.

Her school was building a pool and insisted all the girls had to learn how to swim before it opened. For Helen and her friends, their idea of swimming was to go down to the Jersey shore and bounce up and down in the waves.

But without a pool to practise in their lessons were a little unconventional, to say the least.

Once they were all suited up in their cossies, their teacher asked the girls to lie down on long benches and practise their strokes. They were mortified. Let's face it, no matter how cute your swimsuit is, there is nothing remotely attractive or graceful about flailing your arms and legs about while perched on a bench.

Finally the big day arrived but Helen's debut was not quite what she hoped for. Once her woollen suit soaked up the water, no amount of fancy breaststroke was going to keep her afloat.

Doris said she often chuckled at the thought of her mother-in-law jumping enthusiastically into the pool and promptly sinking.

Horse racing was a passion for Mona Collins and she would never miss a meeting. A longtime member of the Australian Jockey Club, rain, hail or shine every Saturday Mona could be found intently watching the thrills and spills from the Members Stand at Royal Randwick in Sydney.

Always dressed to the nines, Mona's favourite accessories were a stylish but very practical pair of Ferragamo flats and her lizard-skin handbag.

The only thing Mona didn't like about race-day fashion in the 1970s was wearing a hat. But when she saw this dandelion yellow coat dress from Italy on the 6th floor fashion salon at David Jones, she had to concede that some outfits deserve that little extra effort.

It's easy to imagine this flamboyant 1926 beaded dress being worn by a wild and glamorous flapper to dance parties and all that jazz. But when Betty Sturbridge gave Doris this dress, it seems it had had a mysterious secret life.

Betty and her sister found this exquisite treasure hidden in the bottom of a trunk in the attic after their mother died. They were astonished because they had never, ever seen their mother wearing anything remotely glamorous and certainly nothing like this. She had been a hard-working nurse all her life and the girls rarely saw her out of uniform.

Betty's mother had never mentioned the dress and none of her friends remembered it, but it must have been very special to her to have kept it for so long.

They would never know why but Betty was delighted to discover that her practical mother had kept such a delicious secret.

My mother was in an utter quandary about what to wear when she received an invitation to dine with the captain of the *QEII*.

Having carefully read the 'Information for Passengers' guide discreetly tucked behind the vase of flowers in her stateroom, she was relieved to see there was a hair salon on board and that babysitting services for my brother, sister, and me could be arranged with the delightfully named 'Nursery Stewardess' or 'Bedroom Stewardess'. But the dress code for dinner was not so clear.

All the passenger booklet offered was that 'Informal Leisure Wear' was the order of the day and 'Gentlemen who have brought dinner jackets will wish to wear them in the evening, otherwise a lounge suit will be equally suitable'.

Deciding to err on the safe side, Mum put on her beloved 1960s classic navy blue Dior suit. Because, as every woman knows, you can't go wrong in Dior.

Having just returned from a jaunt to the super glamorous Monte Carlo Grand Prix, I thought I knew just what to expect at that other famous car race, Le Mans, in France.

So I dressed the part to cheer on the ace drivers of Ferraris, Porsches and Lamborghinis in a flowery silk Mondi jacket from Italy, sexy white hot pants and a pair of knee-high gold lamé boots.

My date for the weekend had his own plane which he filled with friends - and French champagne - and flew us all straight to the race track. All very exciting until I discovered that two days of rain had transformed the trackside into a sea of mud.

Within two minutes of arriving my boots were ruined. The only compensation was that the remaining gold lamé and legs not splattered in mud still drew lots of admiring glances.

My date was lovely but, like the boots, our romance didn't survive the weekend.

When Annouska arrived in Melbourne from Europe during the Second World War, strict rationing had forced women to make do without luxuries and become creative about keeping up a semblance of style, such as painting seams on their legs in place of silk stockings.

Annouska quickly proved to be even more resourceful and inventive at creating something beautiful out of nothing. After a hard day's work as a seamstress, she would collect all the scraps of fabric on the floor and create wonderful concoctions for herself and her friends - handbags, hats, corsages, even gloves.

From a few scraps of holly red felt, Annouska created this divine appliqué handbag to complement the Rockmans of Melbourne suit she had gone without for six months to buy.

Proof that with a little imagination, a woman of style and substance can always find a way to be impeccably dressed even in the worst of times.

Bertie had a penchant for daring dresses in the 1970s but not enough places to wear them. An invitation to a Halloween fundraising party at her local country club at last gave her the perfect opportunity. Determined not to be outshone by anyone, Bertie chose a slinky cream jersey Halston, held together just so by a strap over one shoulder.

Feeling impossibly glamorous and bold, she arrived in high spirits with her friends to be greeted, somewhat to her dismay, by a group of twelve nuns from the local diocese. Not being a regular churchgoer, Bertie didn't recognise the nuns and was a bit taken aback that her wild night out was going to be a drag because she'd have to behave properly.

As the night wore on and the champagne flowed, she gradually became a little less self-conscious. Then, when the party moved out to the pool, the unthinkable happened.

In a flash, the nuns disrobed and jumped naked into the pool. That was shock enough, but then Bertie and her fellow partygoers registered an even bigger surprise - the nuns were all men.

Free at last to misbehave, Bertie nevertheless kept her lovely Halston on and had the time of her life.

From injecting punk into fashion in the 1970s with then-partner Malcolm McLaren of Sex Pistols fame to being honoured with an OBE, Vivienne Westwood is a true original. And trying to categorise Vivienne Westwood's designs is, as she herself once said, like trying to get a ship into a bottle. And a little like trying to shoehorn yourself into one of her fabulously skintight creations.

Westwood's resolutely non-conformist, highly theatrical and often outrageous designs may have influenced fashion for more than three decades but her creations have never been for the faint-hearted.

Once described as 'Marie Antoinette meets the power suit', this 1990s va-va-voom purple velvet and wool bodice and skirt, with a cheeky flurry of tulle escaping front and centre, is a classic example.

Long hostess gowns were all the rage for entertaining in the 1970s and Lunetta Headley loved them so much she had one in just about every colour.

As Lunetta believed brighter and bolder was better, this stunner printed all over with tropical flowers was a firm favourite. A souvenir of her parents' travels, the label reads 'Meredith of Hawaii'. And of course it was pure polyester, an absolute must for any fashionable party girl back then.

Doris always thought it was delicious that Lunetta was such a flamboyant dresser, given that her ancestors were the 'plain people' or Mennonites of Pennsylvania who had strict rules about dress, wearing only very simple black or maroon clothing and always covering their heads, no matter if they were inside or out.

Lunetta not only adored bright colours, she loved going barefoot. Apart from being infinitely more comfortable at a pool party, in such an arresting dress who's going to be looking at your feet anyway?

In the 1960s Joanne and Vernon Buller loved to show off their beautifully restored house in Delancey Street on Society Hill in Philadelphia.

Like many of the city's once grand mansions, in hard times the former home of one of the town's wealthiest families had suffered the indignity of being converted into a cheap rooming house, but the structure had remained sound. No expense had been spared in restoring the house to its former glory, even to matching the original paint colours and trim for each room.

Joanne adored the house but the only problem was that the ceilings were so high and the rooms so large that it was almost impossible to keep the whole house as warm and cosy as she'd like in winter.

Ever practical, Joanne resigned herself to focusing on heating just one or two rooms and adopting a layered look in the winter months. And it was a perfect excuse to splash out and buy this Rulaine blue wool dress and matching cape so she could look fabulous and stay toasty at the same time.

Doris's good friend Verda Edmiston was the president of a prestigious women's college in Philadelphia in the 1980s. Renowned for her sensible, no-nonsense approach to education and life in general, Verda was no slave to fashion. However, on the eve of the college's centenary, she was stumped over what to wear to the celebrations.

Doris, as always, came to the rescue and offered to lend her this delightfully frothy chiffon concoction from the 1960s, a dress few women could resist. Verda said she wouldn't feel comfortable wearing a dress from another era, but Doris was determined.

Once Doris had worked her magic and convinced her to just try on the dress, Verda was smitten. It instantly made her feel beautiful and brought back memories of carefree summer parties and picnics at her family home in Savannah, Georgia - the perfect frame of mind for a celebration.

And Doris's reward was seeing her friend glowing with happiness and waving regally to the crowd as she was driven around the college stadium in an open-top car.

In the 1920s Mary Edgar Blood majored in Greek and Latin at Cornell University - and fell in love with her future husband.

When Mary later moved to Chicago with her husband, she fell in love all over again with the city's famous jazz scene, dancing until the wee hours in the latest flapper styles like this snazzy lace-panelled party dress.

But while Mary loved her hectic social life, she was no dilettante. A passionate supporter of the underdog, she was a committed human-rights activist and campaigner for women's suffrage. Leading protests in the streets or quietly helping those in need behind the scenes, Mary would be first in line.

One day Mary came out of her house to find people marching down her street in a procession she assumed was a protest march. Always keen to help a good cause, she immediately joined in to find out what the fuss was about.

Mary was enjoying herself until she discovered that she was marching in Al Capone's funeral procession. She ducked out and made a quick getaway.

When Nellie Hanson Hart married into one of the first families of Ipswich, Massachusetts, on the 10th of July, 1860, her wedding dress was not only the height of fashion but admirably patriotic.

Created from no less than twenty metres of the finest silk taffeta, her brown plaid crinoline dress featured fringed, bell-shaped 'Mary Lincoln' sleeves, so named after the fashion set by the wife of Abraham Lincoln, who had just won the Republican nomination for President.

Nellie's new family was so grand that her father-in-law was referred to as 'Henry B. Hart of the Hart Family of Hart House', one of the most stately and historically significant houses in the country. Built in 1640, it was here that townsfolk brought their grievances to the first family, even the shocking charge that one of the Harts was a witch.

Centuries later, two of the original rooms were removed intact and installed in Delaware's Winterthur Museum, renowned for its collection of Americana.

But no matter how grand her new family was, after her big day the ever practical Nellie transformed her bridal gown into her best going-out dress, always guaranteed to turn heads.

Any woman who can pull off a bold red, white and blue printed and flared polyester pantsuit like this would surely have had front row seats at the Astrodome in Houston on the 20th of September, 1973.

It was standing room only for the 'Battle of the Sexes' between tennis champ and notorious male chauvinist, Bobby Riggs, and women's world champion, Billie Jean King.

Bobby arrived at the Astrodome in a rickshaw pulled by scantily clad glamazons, determined to beat 'the women's lib leader', as he called her. Billie Jean preferred to be carried in Cleopatra-style by well-buffed, bare-chested men dressed as slaves.

It was a big day for women's lib, with 30-year-old Billie Jean cleaning the floor with her 55-year-old opponent.

Once word about the brilliant fashion parades my godmother Doris hosted spread, she was inundated with invitations. One of her favourite partners in these events was Deb Haviland, a mover and shaker who loved organising fundraisers in her beloved hometown in Maine.

As Victorian fashion on the East Coast of America was to be the order of the day for Deb's event, Doris dutifully packed her tailored wool suits for men and women, overcoats and capes, hats, gloves and bundles of woollen petticoats.

Normally downright freezing in winter, Maine makes up for it by being pleasantly mild in summer. But the week before the parade temperatures reached a dizzying 95 degrees Fahrenheit, unthinkably hot for Maine. Worried their audience would pass out in the windowless theatre, Doris and Deb hunted down every fan in town - and prayed.

A cool change swept in just in time and Doris's show was such a triumph that Deb gratefully donated this stunning charcoal silk 1920s dress to the collection.

After walking out of Heathrow airport to begin my new life in England in the 1980s, I must have looked like a target for every department store. Within a week of arriving I was bombarded with cards to use at every one in town.

As Patsy in *Absolutely Fabulous*, Joanna Lumley later made Harvey Nichols famous as a shopping mecca but I was already a longtime fan so I decided that would be my first port of call. With my new charge card burning a hole in my pocket, I went straight to the second floor designer department.

There I saw the most spectacular shiny brown raincoat, scattered all over with glittering gold dots.

Living in London's climate justifies buying a special raincoat, so I didn't feel the slightest bit guilty, though perhaps I didn't have to buy one by Robert Nell of Paris for three hundred pounds!

Besides the price, the other thing I very conveniently ignored was the label I read inside the coat: 'Do Not Get Wet'.

Not very practical, but then who in their wildest dreams would get a 'rain' coat this fantastic wet anyway?

Toppy was the apple of her son's eye. Her real name was Margaret but Sam always called her Toppy – the reason has long been forgotten but everyone remembered her larger than life personality and generosity.

Toppy loved entertaining, the theatre and travelling, but she always had time for Sam. No matter where she was going in the evening, Toppy would always read to him. Every summer he remembered her spending hours playing with him on the beach, building sand castles and 'digging for China'.

When Sam went to Yale, Toppy would come up North to visit and throw glamorous theatre parties, inviting Sam and his friends along.

Toppy always looked wonderful but this 1950s party dress was Sam's favourite. Swathed in champagne-coloured tulle and sparkling sequins, his mother looked as if she could make magic happen - and invariably she did.

As a young girl, Doris's friend Audrey had always dreamed of leading a life of luxury and travelling the world. What she had never imagined in her wildest dreams was falling in love with a man who could grant her every wish.

As soon as he met Audrey, Paul Chancellor knew he had found the woman he wanted to spend the rest of his life with. And spoil.

He loved to surprise his beloved wife with gifts like the impossibly beautiful and expensive ring he had specially commissioned for her by an exclusive Bond Street jeweller. When Audrey lost it she was devastated. But Paul simply wrote to the jeweller and had another one made.

Paul also loved to buy Audrey beautiful dresses that he would then insist she model for him, like this glamorous beaded evening dress, perfect for their annual jaunt with friends to Puerto Rico.

But of all the wonderful little things Paul did for Audrey, her favourites were treasures no money could buy - the tender poems he wrote to her.

This Lanz dress was pretty darned glamorous for a young student travelling around Europe in the late 1970s.

During my year abroad in Paris I loved just hopping on a train to somewhere I'd never been before but I refused to look like a backpacker.

So instead of jeans I opted for dresses with matching espadrilles and coordinating handbags (naturally!). And there would be no backpack for me, no matter how practical. Besides, I needed a large suitcase to fit all my snazzy travel ensembles - you never knew who you might run into or what you might get up to along the way.

The look I was going for was sort of Southern Belle meets The Hamptons. Lots of bold colours but nothing too seductive or provocative. This suited my parents down to the ground as they thought it might help keep me out of trouble.

But looking back, there was no way I was going to blend in wearing this dress, especially when the combination of red, white and blue looked awfully like an American flag.

Not all the dresses in my godmother Doris's collection were given to her by women. Some of her favourite dresses and their stories came from men who had loved the women who wore them.

Once, when Doris had finished a talk about the history of fashion at a local university, an elderly man came up and announced that, although he was legally blind and couldn't see the show very well, her stories had put paid to his plans to sneak out early.

'All the time you were on stage you were pretty much a blur and so were the dresses the models were wearing … Even though I couldn't see anything, I could hear your stories and they captivated me. I enjoyed every minute and I just have to tell you this because I hadn't expected to.'

Two days later, this stunning, claret-coloured 1940s lace dress arrived in the post.

Enclosed was a note: *My dear wife wore this dress. It was her favourite. I hope you will tell her story. She was my greatest love.*

As extroverted, glamorous and outrageous as her designs, Zandra Rhodes was undoubtedly one of the leaders of the pack in Britain's audacious new wave of fashion in the 1970s.

Her flare for bold design and innovative construction can be seen in this sexy fitted black wool dress, with its tightly ruched skirt and exposed zip, a recent donation to the collection from photographer Robyn Beeche.

Robyn fondly remembers seeing Zandra for the first time in 1974, launching a line of printed silks for Sekers Silks at a David Jones parade in Sydney, and thinking she looked like a gorgeous Rosella parrot with a rainbow of colours in her hair.

A few years later she began photographing Zandra's collections on the runway and often accompanied her when she presented collections around the world. Zandra was always giving her friend clothes and after eighteen years of collaboration Robyn had amassed a vast archive of her work.

When Robyn generously donated this stunning piece and several other Zandra Rhodes originals, I couldn't help thinking that Doris would have loved to have met Zandra.

For my godmother Doris, the stories behind the dresses she collected were often the real treasures, and the tale of this Edwardian gown was one of her favourites.

Her friend Charles Reid remembered his grandmother Mary Davis as a proper Presbyterian lady who never danced or played cards, but went to all the dances dressed in the most exquisite gowns such as this dove grey wool day dress with intricate lace, net and silk cord embroidery. She loved to sit at the edge of the dance floor and talk to everyone at the party.

Like Mary, her youngest daughter, Eveline, enjoyed a good chat. She was a spontaneous, effervescent girl, very popular and socially inclined but, at 14, not a very good student.

When Mary asked her, 'Eveline, why can't you do as well in school as Kate Bogel does?'

Eveline replied quickly, 'Well, in the first place, Kate has a very intelligent mother.'

Mary thought it best to change the subject at that point.

Typical, I thought, you always meet the man of your dreams just when you're leaving town. In this case I had just completed a year studying in Paris and was about to return to the United States in three days when I met Frederic in a French cafe.

But what do you wear to Paris's coolest basement jazz club, Le Caveau de la Huchette, especially when your date is the hottest Frenchman you have met in a year?

Not one to let a chance like this go to waste, I spent my last few francs - actually, lots of francs - on this super trendy 1990s leather Valentino skirt with stars stitched all over it.

Matched with a silky red blouse, a pair of black velvet Philippe Model ankle boots, and with my hair pulled back into a sassy ponytail, I felt ready for my final Parisian adventure.

We danced all night to the best jazz and my date was *très charmant*. I left Paris on schedule, but with delicious thoughts of what might have been.

D esigned to make an unforgettable entrance, this spectacular blue chiffon evening gown fittingly belonged to a successful actress.

Odette Myrtle, who starred as the first 'Bloody Mary' in the stage version of Rodgers and Hammerstein's *South Pacific* in Chicago in the 1950s, adored entertaining in this outfit. Apart from the obvious appeal of her svelte figure being so elegantly encased in glittering panels of glass beads, the dress's enormous wing-like sleeves are held together over the arm with diamanté-encrusted clips, which allowed glimpses of bare skin to show each time Odette gestured gracefully when greeting her guests or telling a story.

Odette made so much money from playing Bloody Mary that she later opened a restaurant in New Hope, Pennsylvania, just beside the canal, which she called Chez Odette.

Everybody who was anybody had to eat at her restaurant at least once. And Odette relished playing the role of hostess - a perfect opportunity to show off dresses like this.

Born and bred in the English countryside, Ida Heaton lived to ride with the hounds, one of the more energetic highlights of a gentlewoman's social calendar at the turn of the twentieth century.

On the day of a hunt, Ida was always up at dawn and impatient to get to the stables and her beloved bay hunter, Redford, especially so when she was to join the Quorn, one of the world's oldest and most famous hunts.

Dating back to 1696 and named for the village where the hounds were kennelled, the Quorn Hunt ranges over a vast area of countryside in Leicestershire and parts of Nottinghamshire and Derbyshire.

An accomplished equestrian, Ida had to be even more adept than her male counterparts at handling the rough terrain and negotiating jumps because, in accordance with the decorum of the times, she had to ride side-saddle.

Dressed in a superbly fitted dark grey tweed riding habit with veiled satin top hat, gloves and riding crop, Ida was the picture of ladylike elegance - as one should be when one rides with the Quorn alongside the Prince of Wales.

As the wife of an American diplomat in Luxembourg in the 1960s, Betsy Harvey's life sometimes seemed like one endless party to her friends at home.

But while Betsy took her role very seriously, her letters to Doris about the ups and downs of everyday life in her lofty social circle proved she remained delightfully down to earth.

'Before the palace reception there was a curtseying rehearsal at the Embassy Residence. Only three of us were old hands. All the others had talent, with the exception of the wife of the new attaché, who had absolutely no sense of balance and couldn't put one foot behind the other for some reason.

'There were so many of us in line at the reception, however, that she was held erect as she went through the ordeal of curtseying to the Grand Duchess and I guess no one noticed an embarrassing wobble. Fortunately, the American ladies only go halfway down, sort of like a little girl's curtsey in slow motion, whereas a practised European sinks gracefully to the floor surrounded by a gorgeous pouffe of skirt.'

At least in this ethereal blue gossamer evening gown, Betsy herself would never be anything but graceful.

This exquisite velvet Belle Epoch handbag was one of my godmother Doris's favourites, as much for the story behind the woman who created it as for its beauty.

It was a gift to Audrey Chancellor from her sister-in-law Asta Girey. Forced to flee Russia in the late 1800s, young Asta ended up stranded in Hong Kong without a passport. But as Asta's ethereal beauty never escaped notice for long, she found an obliging Englishman to agree to a hasty marriage of convenience and passage to France.

Soon after arriving in Paris and divorcing her rescuer, Asta found work as a companion to a French lady and put her unerring sense of style to work designing accessories for her. When her exquisite handiwork came to the attention of Alexandrine de Paris, she was commissioned to design gloves for their elite clientele.

But the ultimate accolade came from the House of Worth, and before long Asta was designing handbags like these and many other beautiful necessities under the famous label.

When she wasn't designing accessories for grand ladies, Asta loved to paint *en plein air* on the banks of the Seine.

Having spent her early married life constantly moving from one rented house to the next, Doris dreamed of finally unpacking her books and hanging dresses like this 1970s Lola Kay of Belgium original in a real wardrobe.

To her, that would mean she was finally 'home'.

Over cocktails one evening, friends Edith and Lovett Dewees suggested Doris and Howard take the plunge and design their own house.

So they did. They found three acres on a hilltop in rural Pennsylvania with a lane leading down to a stream, and built their dream home. Their children all grew up there, and as the years passed the family always came back together there. Doris said she always blessed her friends for giving them the courage to take that first big step.

And of course to finally enable her to have a wardrobe she could fill with her precious clothes.

This Edwardian dress belonged to a lovely young Japanese girl, Yuko, whose parents worked as servants for a wealthy Maine industrialist and his family in the early 1900s.

When Yuko's parents decided to return to Japan, their employers asked if they could adopt Yuko and bring her up in America. Her parents were torn but they eventually relented because they knew the family loved Yuko like a daughter and could offer her more than they ever dreamed possible.

Yuko grew into an accomplished and beautiful woman who had many suitors. Soon after she married though, tragedy struck when her young husband died suddenly. But as he had left a small fortune to Yuko, the grieving young widow was soon pursued by an even longer line of suitors.

It wasn't until Yuko met writer Simon that she decided to remarry. She knew he was the one and, soon after, they married and moved to Illinois. Yuko did this without the blessing of her family, however, who dismissed Simon as 'a no-account writer' who was only after her money.

Many years later when Yuko died, Simon created a tranquil garden area he called Yuko Park to house a Japanese-style monument in memory of the woman he adored. The monument to his true love is still standing today.

Of all the fashions of the 1960s, the paper dress was not meant to be taken seriously. The Scott Paper Company invented it in 1966 solely as a marketing gimmick. For one dollar, women could buy a paper dress and receive coupons for the company's other paper products.

But when half a million women flocked to buy the paper dress and the fashion world caught on, an exciting new trend was born. Convenient, cheap and chic, soon just about everything wearable was paper, from underpants and bell-bottoms to waterproof bikinis and raincoats. There was even a paper dress you could grow herbs on when you added water!

Delores Brooks loved the idea of being able to afford a whole new wardrobe in all the coolest new prints. Her favourite was this mini dress with a 'Florentine paper' effect, but she also had a paisley print and a funky psychedelic paper dress. She loved the convenience too - her days of lugging suitcases full of bulky clothes were over.

The inevitable limitations of clothing that ripped or disintegrated after a few washes ended the reign of the paper dress a few years later. But this dress is a reminder of the creative innovations of the 1960s, when Delores was not the only one willing to embrace something new and different.

Every morning on the way to work, Augustine Ralston's favourite ritual was trawling her local news stand for the latest women's magazines. A skilled dressmaker, Augustine loved browsing the fashion pages for couture designs she would then masterfully conjure for herself.

An article in a 1910 issue of the *Ladies' Home Journal,* 'Clothes for Women who Study Economy', had given her an idea for a tailored and sophisticated suit to wear that autumn.

Inspired, Augustine went immediately to work on a bolt of black pinstriped wool she had been saving, expertly cutting and tailoring it to shape, adding jet beaded appliqués from one of her mother's old suits.

She dithered over a removable chemisette and cuffs on the sleeves but in the end she opted to keep it simple, recalling the *Journal*'s advice that 'there is economy in selecting styles which are simple and good in themselves, as they remain in fashion far longer than the much-trimmed type'.

But she just couldn't resist adding an extra flourish of lace on the sleeves - the last word in simple elegance.

I just had to have these cutting-edge Italian shoes after reading Ayn Rand's *The Fountainhead* one summer.

Written in 1943, it's the story of brilliant young architect Howard Roark and his uncompromising take on modern architecture. He has a passionate love affair with a beautiful woman, Dominique Francon, who tries to destroy him - the perfect summer read!

I fell in love with the ideal of Howard Roark - a strong-minded man who rebelled against the strictures of classical architecture and instead saw beauty in clean, austere lines, walls of glass and steel and towering skyscrapers. I found myself daydreaming about meeting a man like him for a romantic dinner in the penthouse of one of his skyscrapers.

As I browsed in a shoe shop later I thought of what I would wear - a tailored jacket, nipped tightly in at the waist, a pencil line skirt and - wow, these shoes! With dramatic gold steel rods for heels, they were architecture for the feet - modern and unique, just like a Howard Roark building.

Whenever I wear them, I spare a thought for my literary hero.

Wendy Batson was strolling down Kensington High Street in London when the sight of this distinctive 1970s Jean Muir dress in a thrift shop window stopped her in her tracks.

From the trademark pared-down look, the perfect drape of the silk jersey and the voluminous sleeves, she immediately knew it was classic Jean Muir and she just had to buy it for her friend Doris.

Doris was over the moon to have a Jean Muir original in her collection. But ironically she soon found that the audiences at her showings of the collection preferred dresses from earlier eras. The 1970s was still too recent for them.

All these years later anything from the 1970s is decidedly vintage and sought after. And, as Jean Muir couture is hard to find, this dress has become one of the collection's most popular and valuable pieces.

Lucky for me, it also fits me like a glove. I chose it over all the thousands of other dresses in the collection to wear for a photo shoot for *Grazia* magazine.

In the 1870s, little girls were dressed like miniature adults with all the trimmings - bustles, bonnets, capes and buttoned boots.

While they often looked almost as elegant as their mothers, it must have been difficult being a corseted mini-me reflection of your mama when you'd rather be climbing a tree. But if the outfit was as becoming as this red wool dress with velvet trim perhaps it would have been worth the sacrifice.

This gem was unearthed by one of Doris's friends, Ebbie Greene, in an attic overflowing with trunks full of clothes worn by generations of her relations.

That the buttons were missing from the little dress made it all the more precious in Doris's eyes for the story it told of the times. Buttons, made by hand from wood, shell and glass, were so expensive in the nineteenth century that the ever practical Victorians commonly removed them from one dress to be recycled onto another.

Doris liked to think the mother-of-pearl buttons she saw on a little velvet jacket Ebbie also passed on to her might have come from the red wool dress.

On hot and humid days in Palm Beach when only something flowing and light would do, Sidney Kendall loved to wear this silk batik kaftan printed with butterflies in delicious sherbet colours.

Sidney lived on the East Coast of America but had always spent her holidays in Florida. When her two beloved grandchildren were old enough to travel on their own, she treated them to an all-expenses-paid vacation to the beach every summer.

Renowned for her forthright nature, Sidney was one of my godmother's favourite people. As Doris wrote to another friend, 'There is no question you always know where you stand with her, which is an advantage and a disadvantage from time to time. I have been the object of her generosity more than once and I am grateful for it.'

This divine 1970s classic was one of the many generous gifts Sidney gave Doris.

It's a truth universally acknowledged that fashionable doesn't necessarily mean comfortable. This was never truer than in the late nineteenth century when a lady's figure was laced into submission with whalebone and watch-spring wire.

A truly dedicated Victorian fashionista dreamed of wearing the latest creation by master couturier, Charles Frederick Worth, whose gowns were always meticulously fitted and swathed in layers of the finest silk and brocade.

But to achieve the perfect silhouette required of a Worth gown, she must first be encased in a fiendishly tight corset and cage petticoat like this. That ceremony alone was not for the faint-hearted. Along with a strong constitution and a talent for holding her breath, a lady needed a maid with a firm grip and a solid bedpost handy to stay grounded.

By 1881 scions of London society like Viscountess Harberton had formed the aptly named Rational Dress Society to encourage women to abandon restrictive corsetry in favour of boneless stays and fashions that didn't deform the body. One of its radical new rules was that no woman should have to wear more than seven pounds of underwear!

As scintillating as a wasp waist looks with a bustle, I bet most women couldn't wait to be set free.

Having spent more than forty years as an advisor to New York's Japan Society, Mari Eijima was a great supporter of all things Japanese.

She especially loved clothes by Japanese couturier Hanae Mori and the unique textiles she created to use in her stunning designs.

Hanae Mori was the first Japanese woman to present her collections on the runways of Paris and New York, and to have her fashion house admitted as an official haute couture design house by France's *Fédération Française de la Couture.*

This long, slender-fitting 1960s Hanae Mori 'hostess gown' was one of Mari's favourites. Made of divinely slinky silk velvet, it features traditional Japanese designs of waves, mountains and chrysanthemums.

While Mari later owned many designer dresses, she treasured this one because it was her first.

In the 1920s Edith Dewees and her friend Alice Hamilton were determined to venture where no woman had gone before on their overseas travels.

But after months of tramping through the Russian countryside and staying in modest hotels, they were more than ready for a bit of luxury - and an excuse to wear something glamorous, like this wickedly slinky flapper dress.

When the two arrived in Vienna, they decided to splurge on a room at the best hotel in town. As they were ushered into their luxurious suite, the girls were delighted to see they had a balcony overlooking the square. Desperate to wash their clothes after all their adventures, at last they had the perfect place to hang them out to dry. True luxury!

But they were rudely awakened at six o'clock the next morning by a highly indignant concierge hammering on the door. He told his guests in no uncertain terms that it was 'an outrage' that such a prestigious hotel had underwear hanging on the balcony and to remove it at once.

Secretly delighted that they had caused a scandal, the girls fought to stifle an attack of the giggles as they retrieved their clean - and perfectly aired - clothes.

S tylish and original, this yellow raw silk dress with a diamanté collar always reminds me of my first mentor, Florence.

Florence worked at Jane Chalfont's, an exclusive boutique in West Chester, Pennsylvania, where I worked on and off after I left school.

Always unfailingly polite and impeccably coiffed, Florence dressed so elegantly that she was a walking advertisement for the boutique. Everyone wanted to dress like Florence and customers flocked to seek her advice on what they should wear - and hope a little bit of her *savoir faire* would rub off on them.

So I felt honoured when she took a liking to me, a shy, fashion-mad eighteen year old.

Florence impressed upon me the importance of respect and good manners. She also helped me learn the art of accessorising and made me repeat after her: 'Less is more.'

Her innate sense of style meant she could transform any outfit by adding the right hat or shoes and making it her own.

This stunning 1900s lapis lazuli and silver necklace was Astrid Bevan's most treasured gift from her beloved husband, Berkeley.

A mining engineer who had to travel constantly for his work, Berkeley made up for his long absences by seeking out a unique gift for his lovely wife on each trip.

While Astrid awaited his return, she busied herself with all the activities of a wealthy Belle Époque gentlewoman - riding her hunter in Hyde Park, lunching at Claridge's with friends, popping around the corner to her haberdashers, Harrods, to pick up silk and wool threads to finish her latest embroidery.

Her husband had spoiled her with many presents over the years but this lapis from the mountains of Afghanistan was the finest - and the most romantic. Berkeley said the stone symbolised his tenderness and love for her.

And the effect of its rich, vivid blue against the fine creaminess of her décolletage was nothing short of priceless.

Judith was a spunky, lively woman, ever resilient, and fun to be with. She also had a strong sense of what was right and wrong.

Doris recalls her friend showing all these qualities during an extremely difficult time in her life, when Judith was suing the university where she had worked for twenty years for age discrimination.

Despite a formidable and well-resourced opposition, Judith was determined that justice would prevail and she would win her case. And in the end she did.

Anyone who had seen Judith in full flight defending her rights in this bold print Hardy Amies dress suit would know this was not a woman to be underestimated.

Judith was in good company as Hardy Amies was, after all, Queen Elizabeth's favourite designer.

A bigail was so light on her feet when she danced that one of her many admirers compared her to a nymph.

Just like Lizzie Bennet in *Pride and Prejudice*, her dancing ensemble was a simple but elegant muslin gown and handmade satin dancing slippers.

The most important dance of her life was in 1820 aboard the steamship, *The Monarch*, which sailed up and down the Hudson during the long summer months. It was not unusual for laughter and music to ring out from the ship late into the night, and on such enchanted evenings many young women like her fell in love there on the river - often with their future husbands.

This night, when dashing young Mr George Marino gallantly led her to the dance floor, he vowed to never leave her side, and kept his word.

The evening was so special that Abigail pencilled the date and the steamer's name on the sole of her satin dancing slippers and put them lovingly away as a keepsake.

Having lived through the swinging sixties and the aftershock of the sexual revolution, Wendy's parents wanted to be prepared for anything the seventies had in store, especially when it came to their beloved daughter.

So, concerned that Wendy's wild friends might lead her astray, her parents went to a psychologist to get some tips on how to avoid their little girl becoming a 'hippy'. These were just some of the warning signs they were told to look out for:

- An intense interest in 'funky' art and poetry
- A preference for group love rather than individual love (I'm not at all sure how one's parents would check for that)
- Reluctant to get a job but enjoys spending money and just 'hanging out'
- Boyfriends or girlfriends tend to be of other races and religions
- And, last but not least, unkempt hair and psychedelic patterned clothing - a dead giveaway.

Wendy could certainly never be accused of looking anything but kempt and cool in this totally on-trend seventies number. And what Wendy's parents didn't know wouldn't hurt them.

In the 1930s a luxury cruise was the perfect opportunity for a society lady to show off her wardrobe, from dancing and dinner at the captain's table every night to playing quoits on deck.

So as soon as Dorothy Carmody's husband announced he had booked tickets for them on a cruise ship from New York City to Bermuda, she ordered twenty pairs of handmade shoes.

To Dorothy, shoes were the ultimate accessory, and for this cruise she simply could not do without a complete wardrobe of coloured silk satin and velvet for evening, suede and leather for day.

Only the best would do for Dorothy and to ensure her precious shoes would stay in pristine condition throughout the voyage she also commissioned a custom-made leather travelling box with separate compartments for each pair of shoes.

Upon embarking, Dorothy was delighted to see that the large tag placed on her shoe box showed they were bound for Stateroom 5 on the upper deck - most definitely the best room on the ship for her and her shoes.

There's always one girl at school you remember who stood out from the rest, who dared to be different. For me, it was Mary Ellen, a classmate at Hollins College in Virginia.

Mary Ellen was gorgeous, rich and smart as a whip, although she always joked she only came to college to earn her M.R.S. Degree. Of course she went on to graduate with honours and become an interpreter at the United Nations.

When she wasn't getting perfect test scores or roaring around in her blue convertible, Mary Ellen was stepping out in outrageous outfits designed to shock everyone - and stand out amongst the sea of preppy pastels on campus.

Her favourite was this butter-soft kid leather ensemble, apparently the work of one of Elvis Presley's favourite designers. And it certainly proved to be a showstopper, especially when she wore it to a party at the nearby men's college, Washington & Lee.

Mary Ellen loved the notion that a good Texan girl should not be seen in skintight bellbottoms and a skimpy halter top, nevermind one held together with an easily undo-able bow.

But it would take a brave man to test that theory …

When I lived in London in the 1980s, I got to play fairy godmother to my beautiful best friend, Imogen.

Imogen's flatmate, a devilishly handsome English aristocrat, had invited her to Prince Charles's fortieth birthday party at Buckingham Palace at the last moment after his girlfriend pulled out.

Luckily, Doris had just sent me this glorious black lace dress, embellished with a silk corsage of pink roses, with a note attached saying: 'Just in case something requires a dress like this ...' Well, the something had come.

When Imogen tried on the dress, she looked positively regal, especially when I added earrings, gloves and the master stroke - a tiara fit for a princess.

But three nights before the ball, Imogen's flatmate announced that his girlfriend had decided to accompany him to the ball after all.

So Cinderella didn't get to the palace but at least she got to dine out for years on how she almost did.

When I lived in Lot in France in the 1970s, I met my share of fascinating people. But one of my all-time favourites would have to be the irrepressible Quentin Crewe.

Despite a lifelong struggle with muscular dystrophy, Quentin was a globe-trotting adventurer, a prolific food and travel writer and an incurable romantic who lived life to the full.

When he invited me to stay for the weekend at a house he was renting in a hillside village near Apt, my room was a converted shepherd's hut dominated by a stunning reproduction of one of Andy Warhol's iconic portraits of Marilyn Monroe hanging above the bed.

That night I joined Quentin and a group of his friends under the stars for an unforgettable dinner. Confit du canard, salad niçoise and fresh goat's cheese, washed down with more than a few glasses of perfectly chilled rosé, never tasted so good.

My sleek 1970s maxi dress with its bold mod flower print was just the thing to wear in the presence of what of course turned out to be an original Warhol.

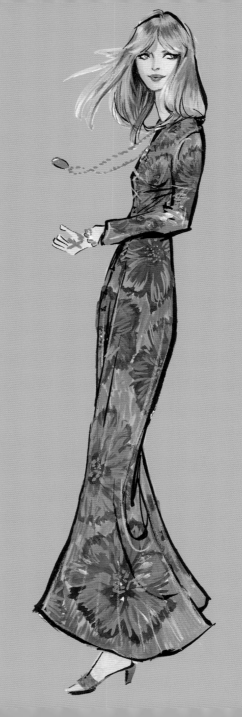

An offer to spend the weekend on the Isle of Capri to celebrate my birthday was too good to refuse. A luxury suite at the Capri Palace with a balcony overlooking the sea, the best food and wine, plus a trip to see to the legendary Blue Grotto, what more could a girl ask for?

Well, that would be my birthday present, a tomato-red linen Versace suit with a matching pair of towering heels. Dressed to the nines, I was set for a bit of sightseeing - or so I thought. But when I saw a little motorboat bobbing away at the pier I was not so sure.

After clinging somewhat desperately to the side as we zipped across the water, I soon discovered getting to the entrance of the Blue Grotto was the easy bit. Getting in was terrifying.

From the motorboat, we had to clamber into an 'owl and the pussycat' rowboat and were told to duck as our 'captain' navigated under an impossibly low and narrow archway in the rock face. After a heart-stopping moment lying on the bottom of the boat, we suddenly found ourselves in the grotto.

The breathtaking sight of the magical blue cavern glowing inside made it all worthwhile. But I made a note to do a little more research before the next must-see adventure.

A coal miner's daughter from Ohio, Leah grew up in the 1950s dreaming of becoming an actress. At high school, Leah's budding talent was noticed and she was offered a coveted scholarship to an acting school in New England.

While there was no doubt Leah was gifted and pretty, she had one drawback that bothered her and bothered others, especially when it came to offering her lead roles. She had prominent buck teeth.

A wealthy friend of the family's asked privately if they thought Leah would be offended if she offered to pay to have her teeth straightened. On the contrary, Leah was of course thrilled - and deeply touched that someone would offer to help her.

For the rest of Leah's life, Isobel was her fairy godmother. From this first act of generosity to opening doors for Leah as she battled to win parts, her benefactor was always there for her.

In turn, there was nothing Leah wouldn't do for Isobel. When she was paid for her first role in a play, Leah went straight out and spent the first money she had ever earned on the most expensive and beautiful crocodile skin handbag she could afford for her fairy godmother.

Lucy Clark's grandmother was married to a Boston Brahmin. As descendants of the English Protestants who founded the city of Boston, the Brahmins were also known as the First Families. As such, they were also the first to be invited to important society events.

Lucy remembers that when her grandmother passed away, the family found trunks of beautiful gowns that her gran had worn to the many glittering events she attended over the years. And as a special treat young Lucy was allowed to choose one to remember her by.

It was not easy, but Lucy finally settled on this bustle dress from the 1880s because she loved the delicate lily of the valley pattern woven into the silk.

It reminded Lucy of her grandmother taking her around the garden as a child to learn the names of all her flowers. She loved the lily of the valley best, not just for its simple beauty but for its unforgettable fragrance.

After one of my godmother's popular 'living fashion' talks about her collection, a man turned up on her doorstep with a mysterious parcel tucked under his arm.

Doris never forgot what he said when he handed over his precious package: 'I have been holding on to this dress, which my wife adored, ever since she died … It's been under the bed gathering dust but still I just couldn't give it away. She loved this dress and I loved her in this dress.'

There was no doubt the blue silk cocktail frock was irresistible and, after he left, Doris just had to try it on. It fit perfectly so she had a photograph taken of her in it and sent it to him with a thank you note.

Soon afterwards she received a letter back saying: *I am so glad you have the dress. You really do it justice.*

Doris would always refer to it as her 'out of the blue' dress, for the way it – and its sweet love story – came to her.

The old saying that it's never too late was certainly true for Frank Cope. When Frank stayed with Doris and Howard for a high school 50th reunion, he confided that he had fallen for a woman who vowed to never marry again after a tragic first marriage. He was determined to convince her to change her mind. Frank was 68, and very patient.

Five years later Frank came and stayed again with Doris and Howard. This time he brought his new wife, Elizabeth. She had finally agreed to take the plunge and marry him and they were blissfully happy.

Frank loved to spoil his wife, so he bought this fabulous navy taffeta cocktail dress for Elizabeth after seeing it in a shop window in Allentown, Pennsylvania - just the thing to wear with her magnificent sapphire engagement ring.

Kathryn James fell in love with William Bernard when they were both students at Harvard University in the early 1900s. All the most romantic moments of their courting days would come rushing back to Kathryn whenever she took out this floaty chiffon dress - picnics, garden parties, long carefree weekends, not to mention William proposing.

By the time they became firm friends with Doris and Howard many years later, Kathryn and William had enjoyed a long and happy marriage. Doris loved that they were so obviously still mad about each other. In the last weeks of her life, Kathryn wrote love poems to William and hid them in the books beside her bed. This one had special meaning for him:

Time is running out
Not in the world
Only for my life
Schedules will soon become a mockery
Will I know what to hold onto
Or must all first be relinquished
To leave some thread of love
In my beloved family

As William later wrote to Doris, his beloved Kathryn had indeed left a powerful thread of love.

P hoebe Fredericks's husband bought her a Degas original, a sublime oil painting of horses at the start of a race, rendered in rich greens, blues and browns.

Unfortunately, the greens didn't go with the green upholstery in the room where she planned to hang the painting. So she returned the Degas to the gallery.

Feeling quite pleased with herself - she had just saved her husband a few million dollars, after all - Phoebe went straight to Saks Fifth Avenue in New York and bought this ritzy Victor Costa suit.

Since Phoebe was leaving for London on the Concorde in the morning she needed something especially extravagant looking to wear and this 1980s suit, with its bronze metallic thread and mink cuffs, was just the thing.

She dithered over buying a mink hat to wear with it but decided the decadent cuffs on the suit were quite enough.

For most of us, dreaming of owning a Chanel original is as good as it gets. But for Anne, the daughter of a wealthy Boston family, her dream come true in 1937 in the form of a wedding gown custom made for her by Chanel.

Cut from the finest lace and silk satin so soft it's almost liquid silver, this breathtakingly beautiful gown hugged every curve and line of the bride's svelte figure, flowing out gracefully into a luxurious train.

A devout Catholic girl, Anne chose to hold her grandmother's precious rosary beads in her hands instead of the traditional bunch of flowers.

Born and bred in an elegant four-storey townhouse in one of the most exclusive parts of Boston, Louisburg Square in Beacon Hill, only the best would do for Anne, including her groom. Like her, he was educated at the best schools in New England and spent summers on Nantucket Island at the family 'cottage'.

Friends of the Bouviers and Kennedys, Anne may have moved in a glittering circle but a Chanel wedding dress, especially one as spectacular as this, would have still made her friends green with envy.

There is nothing worse than feeling overdressed or underdressed on a first date. When a charming Englishman asked me out to dinner in New York, I decided that because it was a week night casual was the way to go. So I chose a white muslin peasant shirt embroidered with flowers - so hip in the 1980s - a blue cotton miniskirt and my favourite thigh-high red suede boots.

I thought I looked totally cool until my date arrived wearing a dapper navy pinstripe suit that looked like it came straight from Savile Row, a polka dot handkerchief in his jacket pocket and polished black bespoke shoes.

To make me feel even more underdressed, instead of grabbing a taxi, he escorted me to a magnificent white Rolls Royce, complete with uniformed chauffeur, champagne on ice and crystal glasses waiting inside.

As I was swept away for dinner at '21', my date was much too gracious to say anything, but I remember trying in vain to pull my skirt down a little and the slightly startled glances from other diners as I walked in on his arm.

According to *The Australian Women's Weekly*, 'the look for 1948 is ladylike ... the effect is come-hither, not here-I-come'. Ellen Christian was not at all sure about this.

For Ellen, fashion was all about making an entrance and she planned on turning more than a few heads at the local dance in this very full and flirty woven raffia skirt.

The only problem with being ahead of the rest with the latest fashion is that Ellen could never have predicted how uncomfortable woven raffia was to sit on, especially on a hot and steamy Brisbane night.

But that gave her the perfect excuse to stay on her feet and dance with every handsome man in the room.

M anly and Violet Whedbee fell in love the first day they met. They were both just sixteen.

Violet's family lived in her great-great-grandfather's Maryland mansion, built when Thomas Jefferson was president. It was a gracious stone house, sitting high on a promontory overlooking the Potomac River, with a grand portico and huge sash windows.

Manly's family lived in a beautiful rose-coloured brick mansion on the other side of the river - exactly opposite Violet's house - with gracious formal lawns sweeping down to the river's edge.

When they were engaged in 1921, Manly solemnly promised Violet that he would buy her a beautiful piece of jewellery from Tiffany & Co every year to mark the anniversary.

For their first anniversary, he dutifully kept his promise with this diamond and onyx bow brooch.

A present in a turquoise box tied with a black satin ribbon has been a family tradition ever since.

This simple but stylish brown silk dress was worn for special occasions by a young Quaker woman in Philadelphia in the mid-nineteenth century.

While Quaker women prided themselves on not following fashion and preferred muted brown, black or mauve fabrics with little or no decoration, this gown shows that didn't mean you couldn't dress with style.

Made from expensive polished silk, expertly gathered into a tiny waistline, with tin buttons covered in velvet, this dress is typical of the more elegant styles worn by the Quaker women in Pennsylvania at the time.

But a practising Quaker in Maryland would opt for a much simpler dress, made from modest silk with far less yardage and only plain glass or wooden buttons. The effect would have been far more subdued.

If I had been a Victorian Quaker, I know which side of the Mason-Dixon line I would have chosen.

In 1934, my mother was taken to Simpsons on Piccadilly in London to choose her first party dress. She was all of three years old.

I doubt Mum had much say in it, but she adored her flowery silk organdie party frock, so much so that she couldn't bear to part with it. When she finally outgrew it, the precious dress was packed away in a trunk in the attic of my grandmother's house.

When I was three, the dress was brought out and I was photographed happily wearing it. When my sister Sarah turned three a few years later, she followed tradition and also posed cheerfully in the dress. Of course it helped that when my sister and I were growing up party dresses for little girls were the thing, the more princess-y the better.

But by the time my sister's daughter, Fiona, was presented with the dress when she was three, tastes had changed. Fiona looked decidedly unsure, as did my daughter, Olivia, when it was her turn to wear it.

Still, just in case the party dress look comes back, our family heirloom is safely in the collection waiting for the next generation of three year olds to wear it.

This Quaker bridesmaid dress was only worn once, in 1870, after it caused a scandal.

Kay Taylor's great-grandmother Verity was just sixteen when she wore this to an unusually elaborate Quaker wedding and unwittingly unleashed a chorus of disapproval.

Made of the finest silk, which cost six dollars a yard - a fortune at the time - it was luxurious by any standards. But it was not the silk, the cost of the wedding or Verity's behaviour that caused the uproar. The problem lay in the trim, the beautiful deep brown silk velvet used to edge the cuffs, collar and bodice. The use of velvet was beyond the pale - too extravagant by far and flagrantly un-Quakerly - and the Elders decreed afterwards at Meeting that the dress could never be worn again.

Out of sight was not out of mind, though, because for years afterwards women talked about 'that dress'. At least Verity got plenty of attention, the mark of a successful outfit.

And Doris's collection gained a pristine piece of history, with a delicious hint of scandal.

Designed to turn heads, this 1930s black lace evening dress forms the perfect silhouette, set off by an elaborate ruffle down the back of the skirt.

It takes a woman of style and substance to pull a dress like this off and Imogen Mason had those qualities in spades. Elegant, confident and a gracious hostess, Imogen was one of those women every young girl dreamed of becoming when she grew up.

Apart from having peerless taste in clothes, Imogen had created a beautiful home, adored her husband and was always there with a comforting hug or reassuring word when her children needed her. But as her good friend Doris observed, while Imogen was the perfect homemaker, she was no homebody.

Certainly no one wearing a dress like this could ever be accused of that. And needless to say, her husband adored her in return …

When Doris retired from her job as the Personnel Director of the American Friends Service Committee, one of the many invitations she took up to showcase her collection was as a guest lecturer on the *Sagafjord* for a cruise through the fjords of Scandinavia.

Unfortunately by the last night of the cruise Doris found she could no longer soldier on - she had lost her voice.

As she whispered to the audience that the parade would have to be cancelled, a man suddenly popped up and shouted: 'No, let's carry on. I'll sing songs instead.'

And so he did. In a rich baritone voice, he sang ditties from the 1920s to the 1950s to go with the vintage outfits. When his daughter-in-law came out on stage wearing this knockout 1940s diamanté-tiered wool dance dress, he gleefully belted out Glenn Miller's 1940s *In the Mood*.

The show was a roaring success and Doris was delighted to discover her rescuer was none other than Carroll O'Connor, star of the 1970s hit television series *All in the Family*.

As any actor worth his salt would say: 'The show must go on'.

A nnie Burnham loved to paint and was inspired by the pre-Raphaelite pleasure in detail, not only in her art but also in her choice of heavenly gowns.

Annie preferred American to French designs because they were more demure, and less ornate, and looked best on her dainty figure. Made of the finest lawn, printed cotton or gossamer silk, often featuring delicate lace panels and satin bows, her Edwardian dresses were works of art in themselves.

Luckily for Annie, her father was wealthy enough to indulge her tastes and she was one of Philadelphia's most fashionable young women.

Her favourite evening dress was this luxuriant silk satin peach gown because it became almost luminescent in candlelight. Annie would wear it with her hair softly coiffed and arrange herself becomingly on the chaise longue to be admired.

At least one gentleman admirer compared her to a masterpiece by Edward Burne-Jones.

The first 'princess of punk', Zandra Rhodes's early passion was textile design but her bold prints were considered far too outrageous by conservative British manufacturers. Undeterred, she opened her own store in West London in 1969 to sell her fabulously funky creations.

For this striking 1980s dress, Zandra combined contemporary art with Chinese traditions. Mixing Vassily Kandinsky's chopstick-like images with versions of Chinese water circles, it was part of a collection she called 'Chinese Constructivism'.

To complete the look, Zandra added diamantés, silk cord appliqués and dramatic billowing sleeves.

What she didn't include is a zip, or hooks or buttons to close the dress - she preferred all her dresses to just 'flow' onto the body.

As va-va-voom as this dress looks, getting it on and off is a major exercise in contortion!

Who would have thought a vintage dress shop at the top of Gold Hill, the ancient cobblestone street in Shaftsbury, Dorset, where almost every Jane Austen mini-series has been filmed, would be the place to find such a divine pair of Bally wedge sandals?

I'd driven into town to buy some bread and cheese for a picnic, but the sight of these espadrilles on a rack outside the shop distracted me and I just had to investigate.

It was as if the shoes were made for me as I slipped into them and laced up the gold ties. So I was feeling very pleased with myself indeed when I later strode up to my friends to show off my snazzy new shoes - until I realised I had come empty-handed.

Luckily, wearing a great pair of shoes usually leads to invitations to share someone else's picnic.

Swimwear for women was never quite the same after Esther Williams, goddess of the pool, dived into Hollywood and onto the big screen with a string of spectacular 'aquamusicals' in the 1940s.

Wearing racy swimsuits in gold lamé or covered in sequins, Esther and her team of tanned, trim and taut synchronised swimmers dived, pirouetted and leapt into the hearts of moviegoers all over the world.

Nicknamed the 'Million Dollar Mermaid', after her role as Australian swimming star Annette Kellerman, Esther caused a revolution in the pool and on the beach as well as the big screen. Swimwear and swim accessories had never been so popular and every woman wanted to look like Esther.

As not everyone can pull off a gold lamé swimsuit at the local beach or pool, many women opted instead for adding a little touch of Esther's glamour by wearing a fabulously exotic flowery bathing cap like this.

Working for an art dealer in New York in the 1980s led to a few unforgettable adventures.

When one of the gallery's emerging young artists invited me to spend a week with him in Umbria, it was an offer too good to refuse. While he painted, I could explore some of Italy's most spectacular countryside. Even better, our visit coincided with the famous *Festival dei Due Mondi* in Spoleto.

As always, Doris came to my rescue with the perfect outfit, a 1910 fitted cream linen and lace suit. After all, I would be following in the footsteps of the aristocratic young Edwardian woman who once wore it on her 'Grand Tour' of Europe.

Sitting with my friend on the lawns at Spoleto, sipping Torgiano Rosso from eighteenth-century goblets and enjoying classical music and poetry readings, I felt like we had travelled back in time.

I remember that day as my little slice of *la dolce vita*.

This spectacular black and white silk-screen printed wool ensemble is the result of three Australian icons meeting in an unforgettable fashion moment.

One of Australia's most celebrated designers, the incomparable Akira Isogawa, was commissioned by Australian Wool Innovation to create a garment celebrating Australian Merino wool.

In turn, Akira drew his inspiration from the work of another iconic Australian designer, Florence Broadhurst, recognised worldwide for her groundbreaking print designs for fabric and wallpaper.

Using one of Broadhurst's trademark opulent prints with hints of the Orient to create this hooded coat and matching shorts, this outfit is a celebration of both how versatile wool is and how effectively Australian designers like Akira fuse so many cultures and influences to create unique fashion stories of their own.

Doris would have been so proud to know that her vision of preserving fashion history has been recognised on the other side of the world.

Even though my mother missed the green hedgerows and buttercups of her beloved England, she loved her life as an expat in Hong Kong in the late 1950s. She and my father enjoyed a busy social life with their wide circle of fellow English and American expats, so when I came along, they decided the best way to celebrate my christening was to throw a party on the 4th of July, American Independence Day.

They booked the dining room at the Happy Valley Race Track for the big event and my mother had a beautiful piece of cream silk printed with large red roses made into a snug and very stylish 'wiggle dress'.

Wearing her favourite strand of Mikimoto pearls and her hair coiffed to perfection by Pierre at the Peninsula Hotel salon, she made a grand entrance with my father, my amah Ming, our dog Lucy and of course me, wrapped in a red, white and blue silk shawl in honour of the day.

Apparently, much to my father's relief, I was a very good baby and smiled the entire evening. I still have my christening certificate and a note from the vicar. He seemed relieved it went well too.

Doris always referred to this unfinished 1880s silk faille dress as a Quaker 'bustle' dress, a contradiction in terms for anyone who knows the ways of the Friends.

Wearing a bustle was out of the question for a Quaker woman because following fashion went against all the principles she had been raised to uphold. Clothing should be plain, sober and modest, free of any vain affectation.

But, as this dress shows, a clever dressmaker could create a faux bustle with voluminous tucking and overlapping at the back of a dress to achieve the same effect - a perfect compromise for the elegant Quaker.

This unfinished dress is a wonderful example of how endlessly inventive women can be at overcoming any obstacle when it comes to looking their best.

D oris's friend Dorothy Steere shared her love of beautiful clothes but usually preferred to wear simple, understated outfits herself.

When a very special occasion arose in the 1960s that demanded something a little more arresting than her usual everyday wear, Dorothy decided it was time to really splurge.

So she suited up and paid a visit to Altman's department store in Boston where she found the perfect solution in this lemon yellow 'watered silk' or moiré sheath dress.

Dorothy said she felt somewhat 'shaken' by the cost, but the dress's beauty and the way it made her feel when she wore it more than justified the price.

Although after that one occasion Dorothy never had the opportunity to wear the dress again, she kept it for years until one day she looked at it in the closet and decided her special dress belonged in Doris's collection.

The special occasion turned out to be her wedding to her high school sweetheart. For Dorothy, yellow was the perfect choice because it symbolised a pledge of faithfulness to the one you loved.

Ruth Epstein loved her James Galanos dress because it was both versatile and simple. Pure 1940s grace and style, beneath the detailed lace bolero is a sexy strapless gown. When the dress was worn with the lace bolero it was perfect for a dinner party - remove it and she was ready to dance.

Although she was the daughter of media tycoon and financier Eugene Meyer, Ruth was determined to contribute to the war effort and also to dress appropriately. As others were forced to make do with so little, it was not the time for shows of extravagance or lavish gowns.

Made from serviceable wool crepe, rather than expensive silk or velvet, she felt her Galanos dress was a suitably understated and practical alternative.

But in the case of someone like Ruth, it didn't matter how simply she dressed, she always looked magnificent.

Esther Burlingham was well known and loved in her hometown in the 1930s for the energy and enthusiasm she put into her work as an elementary school teacher and as president of Santa Fe's garden and landscape committee.

As often as she could, Esther loved nothing better than to combine her passions by taking the children on field trips to teach them all she knew about wildflowers.

So it's not surprising that Esther knew in an instant that she had met her future husband when she discovered that he shared a love of hiking and mountain wildflowers.

When the date was set for her to marry her beloved Jim, Esther made this stylish hat, fittingly trimmed with silk wildflowers, to wear with her going-away outfit.

If any one designer defined the spirit of the 1960s, it was Mary Quant. While she may not have been the one to invent the miniskirt, hot pants or go-go boots, there's no question that her bold combination of pop art and mod style made her distinctive look a worldwide sensation.

From her Bazaar boutique on Kings Road, London, Mary Quant developed the 'Chelsea look' that turned her signature daisy label into the grooviest of groovy brands for young fashionistas in the mid-1960s.

Chelsea girl Daisy Fellowes was a devoted Mary Quant fan and loved to imagine herself wearing the slinky creations actress Diana Rigg made her own as the impossibly sexy Mrs Emma Peel in *The Avengers*.

Daisy loved this mod tie-dye leotard because it was 'so very Mary Quant', with just a glint of Mrs Peel.

In the 1920s Lallie Easterbrook lived with her five older brothers and sisters in a huge mansion in New York City.

Before Lallie was born, the Easterbrooks had purchased the townhouse next door and knocked down the walls to create a home big enough to accommodate their growing family and a grand ballroom to throw the lavish parties they became renowned for.

When Lallie was eighteen, her parents bought her this demure but very fashionable silk dress from a shop in Paris.

Lallie loved how the hem of the skirt was luxuriously full with a ribbon border of gold metallic thread. She had such a wonderful evening the first time she wore the dress she vowed to never get rid of it.

Many, many years later Lallie met Doris, and knew she had found someone who would treasure her dress almost as much as she had.

My daughter Olivia is longing to wear this beautiful dress - perhaps for her eighteenth birthday.

The daughter of wealthy parents and later the wife of a diplomat whose postings took her all over the world, Mithi was used to having hundreds of glamorous outfits to choose from.

Her eclectic wardrobe and effortless sense of style were the envy of all the other wives in the diplomatic service. Mithi not only always looked spectacular, but she carried out her duties as a hostess at countless official dinners and parties with consummate grace and skill.

However, Mithi would have loved nothing better than to spend more time on her passion for sewing, embroidery and dreaming up new designs to wear.

When her husband retired, she made up for lost time by opening her own salon and creating stunning outfits like this blue and gold metallic thread dress for her loyal and wealthy clientele.

It was Valentine's Day 1956 and Mary Kent was sweet sixteen when she fell in love.

The swish cocktail party at her parents' beachfront holiday house in Carmel was in full swing when she caught the eye of a handsome young man, Steve English.

No one noticed as they slipped out of the party later for a romantic rendezvous on the moonlit beach. Wearing her new pink bathing suit, Mary felt wonderfully reckless as they ran into the pounding surf together. It made it all the more exciting that no one knew where they were. Mary knew her parents would have been horrified, but she was not sure if they would have been more upset about her swimming at night or her being out unchaperoned with a young man.

Many years later Mary told Doris that she fell 'truly, madly, deeply' in love that night. And she didn't wear her pink bathing suit again until eight years later when she was on her honeymoon in Venice and had become Mrs Steve English.

Lazing elegantly beside the pool at the Hotel Cipriani, Mary knew her 'vintage' bathing suit was still an eye catcher - even the hotel's waiters were giving her special attention. All the better, her new husband was becoming a wee bit jealous.

Two days after arriving in New York City in the early 1980s, fresh out of college and ready to party, my invitation to a friend's birthday at the ultra-chic Studio 54 seemed too good to be true.

Luckily I had ignored my mother's protests that I would never wear this outrageous red jumpsuit by American designer Norma Kamali. Teamed with my new black ankle boots and a velvet ribbon fashioned into a choker, I was ready for my close up.

My friends and I arrived at Studio 54 in style in a black stretch limousine, as you do, and were whisked past the queue of hopefuls waiting patiently outside.

Inside was wild - dark, loud pounding music, disco balls, trapeze artists swinging above the dance floor and mirrors everywhere, reflecting back cooler-than-cool men in leather, women in skintight jumpsuits, and Grace Jones look-alikes. It was New York on steroids.

My parents were convinced that the crowd who hung out at clubs like Studio 54 would lead me astray. They needn't have worried, though, I was a good girl - although I might have been tempted to buy another Norma Kamali jumpsuit.

When Ellie Simon married Edward Bassett on the 22nd of October, 1910, her bridesmaids looked almost as ravishing as the bride in cream cotton gowns printed with glorious bunches of mauve and pink lilacs.

Ellie had chosen the fabric especially for her sister Lillian because she adored lilacs. According to her well-thumbed dictionary of flowers, lilacs also represented the first emotions of love.

When Lillian wasn't busy designing thimbles for the family business, Simons Brothers, she designed and sold her own jewellery on the side.

When their father died, Lillian took over running the business until she was able to sell it for a healthy profit.

Lillian's business sense was as impressive as her artistry - the proceeds from the sale allowed her to live comfortably and become an artistic lady of leisure.

It's lovely to think there was a time when making thimbles could set you up for life.

W hile many of her girlfriends became slaves to the latest fashions in the 1930s, following fads had never been Jean Harrison's cup of tea.

This demure blue and white polka dot dress with its rickrack trim was as fashionable as Jean would allow.

Jean was a sensible woman, married to a sensible man who was her perfect match in every way, except for his very strange and unconventional first name, Leumas.

None of her husband's siblings could shed any light on the origins of his name and it remained a mystery until Jean discovered the diaries of her late mother-in-law. Apparently his parents could not settle on a name for their baby, their seventh, so they decided to call him Leumas because that was his father's name spelled backwards.

An eminently sensible solution after all.

For many women, accessories are what make an outfit. Ginny McMullin loved wildly colourful and expensive hats more than anything. In the 1950s, in between marriages, she had a boyfriend who would take her to New York and buy her $50 hats, just because he wanted to indulge her.

At the time paying $50 for a hat was above and beyond - and that boyfriend was a keeper.

But if he really cared for Ginny, he had to go one step further because she insisted each hat had to have a matching scarf.

Her favourite outfit was a simple but elegant fawn silk suit. It gave Ginny the ideal canvas to work her magic. Just by adding a different hat and scarf, with her customary flair she could wear it over and over again and no one would be the wiser it was the same 'old' suit.

When Ginny was ready to update her hat and scarf wardrobe, Doris was the very happy recipient of a glorious array of stylish hat boxes filled with treasures in all colours, shapes and sizes.

The night Sarah Emlen was born on the 12th of April, 1861, will always be remembered by her family and countless other American families.

For Sarah was born on the fateful night the Confederate forces fired on the Union garrison at Fort Sumter in Charleston, setting off the American Civil War.

Sarah grew up hearing the stories of her family's role in the Civil War from her father, Samuel, a formidable figure who always carried a walking stick and wore an immaculate top hat. Born in New England, the Emlens were proud to be known as Unionists or North Yankees.

Her parents made a striking couple when they dressed to go out, especially when her mother wore her favourite black velvet bonnet trimmed with ostrich plumes, which set off her fiery red hair and fine porcelain skin.

Sometimes dresses would come to Doris's collection without a story, but in time stories came to them.

This timelessly elegant satin wedding dress with capped sleeves was hanging in a thrift shop window in Hawaii when a friend pounced on it for the collection. Doris always liked to know the tale behind who wore a piece but sadly no one knew who had worn this wedding dress or donated it.

One night, Doris and Howard were watching the classic 1934 romantic comedy *It Happened One Night*, starring Claudette Colbert and Clark Gable, when Doris suddenly recognised her Hawaiian thrift shop number in the famous wedding scene.

While Doris could never say for sure that this was the one and only, to her it would always be her Claudette Colbert dress and bring back fond memories of her favourite film.

And Doris's ever peerless taste of course extended even to her choice of film. *It Happened One Night* was the first film to win all five major Academy Awards - best picture, director, actor, actress and screenplay.

Either way, this is an award-winning dress.

I feel blessed to have had two fairy godmothers. My American godmother, Doris, changed my life by leaving me her priceless vintage collection. My English 'Auntie' Jill gave me another precious gift by teaching me the true meaning of hospitality.

My most vivid memories of her are of the long dresses she wore with big picture hats, presiding graciously over garden parties at her English country house near Plymouth.

When I was six I remember her hosting one in honour of a prominent English politician, Michael Heseltine, who I thought was very handsome. Always the perfect hostess, she had that rare gift for making anyone feel instantly at ease.

Not only that, I was privy to one of her secrets, that she had rolled up her sleeves along with her housekeeper to help provide the banquet for her hundred or so guests. All the vegetables and fruit had come from her precious walled garden behind the house and the pheasant and trout had been sourced from her estate.

Looking back, it seems my English godmother also taught me a thing or two about style and self-sufficiency.

Having arrived in India in the 1940s and spent the next thirty years working there as a teacher, Mary Dunne learned to adapt her wardrobe to cater for the suffocating humidity and monsoonal rains - as well as unexpected invitations. Her secret weapon for transforming any outfit was her enviable collection of exquisite shawls.

During Queen Elizabeth's tour of India in the 1970s, Mary's friend Daphne was to be present when Her Majesty visited a retirement home in Bangalore. But a great 'brouhaha' erupted when Daphne realised she had nothing appropriate to wear.

Mary came to her friend's rescue with her most lustrous shawl, handwoven from the finest silk in America in the 1890s. Now feeling suitably resplendent in her shawl, Daphne waited patiently in the long line hoping the Queen would favour her with a brief nod or smile. Much to her delight, the Queen stopped and chatted to her, the only person to get such royal treatment.

As Mary later told Doris, she always liked to think it was thanks to her gorgeous shawl being fit for a queen.

After I met the writer Sebastian Faulks when he came to see me about renting my house in France, I followed his career closely and faithfully bought every one of his novels.

I was entranced with *Charlotte Gray*, a story about the Resistance fighters during the Second World War, set in a rural part of France not far from where I lived.

Those who could not join the Resistance or fight on the front line found other ways to show their patriotism. Some, like the woman who wore this 1940s black silk dress, chose fashion as their voice. The dress has velvet *fleur de lys* appliquéd all over it, declaring subtly but proudly her love for France.

I like to imagine this woman smoking a cigarette at a party, the picture of casual elegance, knowing her message to her countrymen was written all over her.

Elizabeth Brackett felt very grown up the first time she took the train from Boston to New York City in 1924 at the tender age of thirteen. She rode it alone 'apart from the conductors and other passengers', and her mother met her at Grand Central Station.

Elizabeth's father's ship, the USS *Lakeview* had called in to New York for a brief stop before undertaking minesweeping of the North Sea.

Another exciting first for Elizabeth was riding in a taxi from the station to the docks. But the thrill of the taxi ride paled beside being 'piped aboard' the ship. At the top of the gangplank her father greeted them with open arms and 'more ice cream than I had ever seen in my lifetime'.

Once the welcome was over, her father assigned a handsome young officer to give her a tour of the ship. She was smitten, as much by her guide as the romantic idea of life at sea.

W ho would have thought this to-die-for black evening
gown, with its slinky silhouette and sweeping train,
was created to showcase good old Aussie wool.

Designer Michelle Jank more than fulfilled her brief from
Australian Wool Innovation to create a bold new look to
launch their new Australian Merino and Superior Merino
brands in 2008. Wool has never looked this good.

As part of the marketing campaign to give wool an extreme
makeover, two of Australia's leading fashion photographers,
Georges Antoni and David Mandelberg, joined forces with
Michelle to create an unforgettable showcase of her designs
in the Kimberley Ranges in Western Australia.

Inspired by the wild and dramatic backdrop, Michelle worked
with the models to choreograph staggeringly beautiful images
like this one. In this unique landscape, her designs became
works of art.

This particular work of art is now part of the collection,
thanks to Australian Wool Innovation.

And just because I can't help myself, I tried it on and ... it
fits. I am determined to wear it to the next formal do I get
invited to.

This 1920s silver lamé and velvet cape is one of those spectacular pieces that makes you wish you could travel back to a more glamorous age.

With a Marcel wave in your hair, a beaded evening dress and a glimpse of sleek silk stockings beneath, you would be well and truly ready to paint the town red - and break more than a few gentlemen's hearts.

Along with this divine cape, Doris was given a wardrobe of fabulous flapper fashion like this, including hat boxes full of velvet, lace and silk cloches, by the son of their original stylish owner, Mary Elizabeth.

After meeting Doris on a cruise of the Greek Islands with Howard and seeing her wear some of her favourite vintage pieces, Bob Dyson knew he had found the ideal caretaker for Mary Elizabeth's treasures.

His mother's cape and hats went on to star in Doris's shows all over the world.

If you were young and carefree and living in London in the 1980s, anything could happen, such as my best friend Suzanne and I being invited to attend the spring races at Ascot by a Saudi prince.

The invitation called for some serious shopping, so I went to the poshest boutique I could find in Knightsbridge for an outfit worthy of a prince, and this nifty metallic brocade ensemble by Suzy Peret fitted the bill perfectly.

Suitably glammed up, we spent the day inside the prince's private marquee enjoying his hospitality, which included the prince generously giving us money to bet on each race so we could enter into the spirit of things.

Rather than trying to work out the odds on the riders and horses, we placed our bets using our own very professional method - we chose the best-looking jockeys and the jazziest racing silks.

Our method was hugely successful and we came away from the races with our handbags literally bulging with English pound notes.

The next morning we went straight to the grooviest boutiques in Sloane Street to spend it all.

When Quaker Anna Aubrey wore this pink plaid silk taffeta dress to her graduation ball in the 1930s, it could not have been more different to her mother's graduation gown.

As it was the middle of the Depression, Anna's mother had made her daughter's dress herself from a bolt of taffeta she had been saving for years, waiting for the right moment to use it.

As Ellen stitched away, she smiled as she remembered the dress she wore to her own graduation ball at her Quaker school in 1907.

In those days the matron at the school would go through each girl's trunk and send back home any clothes she felt were inappropriate for a young Quaker lady.

For her, there were no dresses made of silk or featuring any bold red or pink plaid patterns like her daughter's.

Instead she had to wear a white cotton dress with demure sprigs of pink flowers to her graduation ball. But, to her, it was still the most beautiful and grown-up dress she had ever worn.

L ike most women, my mother loved designer clothes but never had the budget to indulge in anything too lavish.

However, living in Hong Kong meant she was able to have something even better: beautiful custom-made clothes created by one of Kowloon's master tailors.

Made by her favourite tailor, Mr Kim, this perfectly cut 1950s tweed suit is completely handstitched, down to the perfectly bound button holes and whisper-soft silk lining.

My mother later told me she was following the sage advice of her favourite designer, Elsa Schiaparelli: 'The perfect wardrobe should consist of a real tweed suit, a travelling suit, a bright red town coat, a cocktail dress, an evening frock and a flannel housecoat - casually tailored in a feminine line ... so it can be worn for intimate dinners.'

And what better reason could a stylish young woman have to order a few more tailor-made ensembles?

Thanks to her fashion bible, *Godey's Lady's Book*, Eleanor's mother knew that every 1920s schoolgirl between the ages of ten and fourteen should have a simple dress for evening wear.

When Eleanor was invited to attend her first big party, her mother resolved to buy something suitably demure on their next trip to town.

Eleanor had other ideas. She was determined to wear a 'proper' party dress with ruffles and bows made from grown-up material like silk or satin, not boring old cotton.

Her mother was equally determined, however. Tears, tantrums and a scolding from her father when he returned home to find his wife and daughter at loggerheads did not deter Eleanor.

Finally her mother relented and bought her this divine, princess-like ice blue party dress, with oodles of ruffles, scallops and the prettiest collar.

From that day on, Eleanor never lowered her standards when it came to party dresses - and was always the belle of the ball.

In the 1930s Eloise Fuller lived in a large stately home, dressed in the latest fashions and went to lots of elegant parties. But after her husband died, the house was too big and lonely so she decided to move to a small apartment nearby.

For weeks she sorted through her wardrobe and gave away all her most beautiful gowns, with the exception of this stunning long peach silk organdie print, and of course her wedding dress.

Beige silk crepe trimmed with clusters of glass bead grapes, Eloise remembered thinking it was the most beautiful wedding dress she had ever seen when it caught her eye at Nan Duskin, a grand store in Philadelphia where all the fashionable ladies shopped.

Eloise couldn't keep it but neither could she let it fall into a stranger's hands. In the end, the only honour she felt befitted a dress so spectacular was to end its life in spectacular style.

And so she did just that. Eloise made an enormous bonfire in her garden and burned it. She later told Doris, 'I gave it a Viking funeral'.

This luscious 1940s cranberry silk crepe belonged to a lovable Quaker maverick who always spoke her mind.

Sarah had one unfortunate problem, however - a tendency to fall asleep and snore at Meeting. It had become so distressing and embarrassing to her that Sarah was at her wit's end and asked her friends Doris and Howard for help.

Howard offered to sit beside Sarah and nudge her if she fell asleep. He did this for three Sundays in a row until Sarah lost her temper and said her own snoring woke her up and she didn't need any help from Howard.

Needless to say, Howard desisted. And Sarah continued to be the picture - if not the sound - of elegance.

After being forced to flee her home in the Dominican Republic as a child, Emily treasured the everyday things many people take for granted.

One night while her family was having dinner, a servant came in and whispered into her father's ear. Her father suddenly put down his cutlery and said: 'I have just had some disturbing news. The servants have suggested we get up from the table, and walk down to the docks as if we are taking an evening stroll, carrying nothing, and go.'

Confused and afraid, the family obeyed and boarded a ship to America, with no money and only the clothes on their backs. It was only later when they heard of the coup that ended American occupation they realised how lucky they were to escape with their lives.

From that time on, Emily learned to treasure everything she was given. She treated every dress she wore as precious and never threw anything out.

If this knockout 1920s flowered chiffon flapper dress, trimmed with cobalt blue glass beads, is any indication, Emily also learned to live life to the full.

Alta Ferguson loved her cluttered home. She had a knack of ending up with everyone else's bits and pieces when they moved house, and although her daughters were horrified she was becoming a sort of pack-rat, she found it comforting and cosy.

Every room was filled with boxes, every table covered, and everywhere you looked there were knick-knacks, vases, lampshades and all manner of treasures she had accumulated. She delighted in the things people passed on to her and saw them as gifts. Often, they were even useful.

When Alta was named 'Woman of the Year' in her home town of Clearfield for twenty years of leading the way in championing local charities, she was delighted to find this elegant 1950s suit of coffee cream lace among her treasures and wore it to accept the honour at the town hall. She felt the elegant brown mink collar gave her a touch of class.

As Alta said of her find for years afterwards, 'a beautiful suit for a wonderful occasion'.

And it goes to prove you just never know when a hand-me-down might come in handy …

Music played a big part in my godmother Doris's life when she was growing up.

The family had a Steinway piano which moved with them wherever they went. Her sister took piano lessons and could play virtually anything. But instead of taking lessons Doris borrowed some of her sister's music books and practised just two pieces over and over, 'Melody' by Schumann and for an encore, Debussy's 'Claire de Lune'.

These two pieces provided Doris with the perfect party trick to free her from what she saw as a thankless chore. Whenever she was asked to perform at a gathering, somebody invariably admired her flawless performance of one of these pieces and asked if she knew any others. After she played the second piece just as beautifully and her audience asked for more, she would modestly say that was enough and it was time for someone else to have the limelight.

Doris reckoned that the person playing the piano was usually stuck there for the rest of the evening and she'd much rather have the opportunity to drift away and meet a handsome man.

And a stunning dress like this would certainly be wasted sitting behind a piano.

American artist Elizabeth Otis Lyman Boott, affectionately known as Lizzie, was brought up in Italy by a widowed father devoted to the wellbeing of his only child. Francis Boott encouraged Lizzie's talent for painting from an early age, moving his household in the 1850s from Boston to a villa outside Florence.

When Lizzie fell in love with her future husband, celebrated American painter Frank Duveneck, the budding affair was cut short - by her father.

Although Lizzie's father admired Duveneck's work, he fought hard for many years to sever ties between Lizzie and Frank. Apart from the artist's inferior social standing, he feared Frank was after his daughter's money. More importantly, he hated to see anybody come between himself and Lizzie.

Novelist Henry James, a close friend of the family, was a frequent visitor to the villa and his letters to Lizzie, her father, and their mutual acquaintances, show he took a protective interest in their happiness.

The tension between daughter and father over Frank clearly caught his writer's imagination and it is said that two of the characters in his most famous novel, *The Portrait of a Lady*, are loosely based on his friends, the Bootts.

An invitation to Henley Royal Regatta, an annual highlight of 'the season' since 1839, is not to be sniffed at. But my excitement gave way to panic when I remembered the strict dress codes for this revered English institution: blazers, flannels, shirts and ties for the men and dresses or skirts with hems down to the knee for the ladies, sensible shoes, hats and gloves.

It was 1980 and my wardrobe consisted of miniskirts, lycra and stilettos. But Granny and her friends came to my rescue.

From Granny I chose an aquamarine flowery dress with a sweet pussy bow and full pleated skirt with a suitably modest hem.

From Daphne I borrowed a snazzy tulle confection of a hat in peacock blue that I'm sure the Queen Mother would have felt proud to wear.

And from Evelyn I borrowed matching gloves and handbag and a pair of sensible shoes even the Queen would have approved of.

All in all, my outfit was the picture of prim and proper, but I was grateful that I didn't run into any of my friends on the day. I just didn't look like me!

After Victoria Brooke married Charles Reed they settled happily in Boston and spent May through September at their summer 'compound' on Cape Cod.

It was said that Victoria and her mother-in-law Eugenie were not only the same statuesque height and build, but they had the same sense of style - at once elegant and dramatic.

Eugenie was so fond of Victoria that she gave her this breathtakingly beautiful gown she had worn to a reception at Kensington Palace in the 1930s. With its intricate floral embroidery work, layers of delicate net and sculpted lace panels, the dress always received rapturous praise whenever she wore it.

Victoria's social life may not have included galas at palaces but she loved showing it off when a special occasion arose or she and her husband entertained.

As for Charles, he always said it was his favourite dress because it reminded him of the two most important women in his life.

J ennifer Johnson described this dusty pink 1950s gem as her 'falling in love' dress and it's easy to imagine why.

With its sweet gingham bow and trim on the hem, it always makes me think of Minnie in Puccini's opera *La fanciulla del West (The Girl of the Golden West)*, and I have no doubt it was a first love or young love.

Since the precious dress and a jaunty matching bolero jacket were handed over with only a shy smile I'll never know the details. But I took the dress home feeling very privileged to have been entrusted with such a treasured piece.

It was a beautiful spring day when I hung the dress and jacket on the line but unfortunately someone else fell in love - our black Labrador puppy, Monty.

When I went out to bring in the clothes that night, I discovered the only remaining part of the bolero jacket sticking out of Monty's mouth.

I was absolutely mortified and this is the first time I have confessed the terrible truth of what happened.

I'm just grateful that the dress survived Monty's affections.

This extraordinary Belle Époque gown belonged to the wife of a Cuban Consul who travelled the world with her husband at the turn of the century.

One of Doris's favourite pieces, the dress came to her after she helped a friend in need. Teresa Ainslee called Doris after her mother, Amelia, passed away, to help her sort through Amelia's trunks of exquisite clothes worn during her time as a diplomat's wife.

Made in Paris, elaborately patterned and embroidered down the back, with metallic tassels swinging gently from the detailed curls of material, this dress would have been worn by Amelia to a formal evening party with her hair swept up into a soft chignon, with simple pearl drop earrings being the only accessory she needed.

After spending a wonderful day time-travelling with Teresa and advising her on the value of some of her mother's clothes, Doris took a station wagon full of treasures to Christie's Auction House in New York.

As a thank you to her dear friend, this is one of several pieces Teresa gave her - the ideal reward for Doris.

One of the many fringe benefits of inheriting a vintage clothing collection is that I can justify spending hours trawling through fabulous old fashion magazines as necessary research. While I of course love looking at the fashions, like Doris I often enjoy the descriptions of the women wearing them even more.

Take this breathless snippet about a new bride in a June 1930 issue of *The American Ladies Home Journal:* 'Mrs Alister McCormick, English gentlewoman to the manor born … in her veins flows the blue blood of the Plantagenets. Now by marriage a member of the distinguished McCormick family, she is the charming young hostess of delightful homes in Chicago and in Santa Barbara.

'Eyes of forget-me-not blue and skin like pink hawthorn blossom … so lovely to see. It is a wonder how its delicate transparency, its clear fresh English colouring can ever survive life on the windy shores of Lake Michigan.'

I'm sure this English rose's delicate hands would have been protected from the icy winters by a sleek pair of suede Hermès gloves like these, purchased in Paris for her trousseau en route to those windy shores.

'Fashion is born by small facts, trends, or even politics, never by trying to make little pleats and furbelows, by trinkets, by clothes easy to copy, or by the shortening or lengthening of a skirt,' Elsa Schiaparelli once said.

And, as flamboyant and outrageous as her chief rival Coco Chanel was elegant and minimalist, Schiaparelli was without doubt one of the most accomplished trend setters, in more ways than one. From collaborations with artists like Salvador Dalí on creations such as her famous 'lobster dress' and the 'shoe hat' now residing in the Metropolitan Museum of Art, to her signature shade of shocking pink, as a designer Schiaparelli was a true innovator, entrepreneur and style icon.

Her recognition as an artist by such luminaries as Marcel Duchamp, Picasso and Stravinsky set Schiaparelli apart from most other fashion designers.

But in the 1950s, all that mattered for women like Dorothy Asquith was that slipping on an exquisite pair of Schiaparelli slingback evening shoes like these with her new LBD instantly made her feel like the most stylish woman at any party.

At the ripe old age of eight, all I wanted was to have a dress no one else had. My yearning to make my own fashion statement stemmed from the fact that my mother loved to make matching dresses for me and my sister, Sarah.

As the younger sister, Sarah wanted everything I had, so my mother made things equal by making us wear the same dresses.

In the many photographs my parents insisted on taking of us holding hands in our matching ensembles, Sarah is beaming and I am looking like the world is about to end.

Luckily I grew out of that phase - and the matching outfits - and now I am delighted if my sister admires what I'm wearing.

Nowadays the two of us love shopping together, although we're not above having a friendly argument about who gets the last blouse on the rack.

We also swap clothes, even though we live oceans apart. For me, living in Australia means Sarah's outfits from last season in America are current season here. So big sister does win out in the end.

Claire was a wild child. With cascades of golden brown curls flowing around her face and down her back, she also looked the part wearing the wildest 1970s fashions.

Printed all over with hazelnuts, chestnuts, almonds and walnuts, she found her favourite nut dress in a funky boutique in Johannesburg.

While Claire was out hunting for the wildest fashions, her friends at college were obsessed with something else that originated in South Africa, the craze of telephone booth stuffing - a competition 'sport' which involved literally stuffing as many people into a phone box as possible.

While Claire might have been daring when it came to showing off her more outrageous outfits, there was no way she was going to risk her precious nut dress in a scrum.

As good Quakers in 1880s Pennsylvania, Sarah and Samuel Elders were gracious hosts who were usually content to offer their guests simple fare.

But for such an important occasion as their daughter's wedding dinner, they decided it was time to serve something special with their homemade fortified wine - a relatively new fangled dessert known as ice cream.

It's just as well Samuel was part owner of a successful lawn mower manufacturing company, as the whole affair turned out to be a costly business - preparing enough ice to keep the special dessert for the Elders' one hundred guests frozen kept the local ice man busy for weeks.

But Sarah knew it was all worth it when she saw the childlike delight on the faces of the bride and groom and their guests when they were served the ice cream.

Some of their Quaker friends were initially unimpressed at such un-Quakerly ostentation but good ice cream has a way of melting away unhappy thoughts.

V alerie knew her husband had an eye for the ladies, but she always believed him when he told her she was the only one.

One day, the receptionist from a ritzy jewellery store in Sydney called Valerie to say her ring was ready to collect. Surprised but intrigued, she went to investigate.

The minute Valerie saw the stone she was suspicious, but she thanked the jeweller and tucked the box into her handbag to inspect the ring more closely when she got home. Sure enough, not only was it the wrong size when she tried it on, but it was an emerald and everyone, especially Valerie's husband, knew she only ever wore diamonds.

So later that evening, dressed in her sexiest negligee and sauciest mules, she put on the ring and prepared for her husband to return from work.

Valerie arranged herself into her most seductive pose on the chaise in the lounge and placed her ring hand just so on her hip to ensure it would be the first thing her rat of a husband would see as he walked in the door...

In 1880 young Anna Mae Dubell lived with her parents in a gracious plantation house, surrounded by white post and rail fences, near Gettysburg.

A true Southern belle, Anna Mae was proud of her family's heritage. Her grandfather had fought in the Civil War with the Confederate Army.

Unlike her rich Yankee cousins who wore brocaded silk bustle dresses and extravagant matching bonnets, Anna Mae preferred wearing printed cottons and embroidered wools, with the simplest of straw hats.

This was her best Sunday dress, made of the finest wool dyed lapis blue and offset with a vibrant paisley trim. When Anna Mae walked to church on her father's arm in this outfit, she felt very ladylike and grown-up.

The day my daughter Olivia and I arrived in London in 2009 just happened to coincide with the famous Harrods sale.

Coming over from Sydney I told myself I was not going because it was far too tempting. But when Olivia discovered our hotel was just around the corner, resistance was futile. We simply had to go - and surely it wouldn't hurt to look?

Temptation of course got the better of me and in less than twenty minutes I was the proud owner of not one, but three pairs of shoes by French designer Roger Vivier.

Couture doesn't come with a better pedigree. Vivier designed for Dior from 1953 to 1963 and we have him to thank for creating the modern stiletto, along with some of the most unique shoe designs in living memory. Vivier's shoes are on display in museums worldwide, including the Victoria & Albert Museum. Now I have three collector's pieces of my own, just in case I have to justify this purchase to anyone.

My favourites are these yellow patent leather sandals, something Twiggy might have worn in the 1970s. Whenever I wear them I remember that wonderful day when Olivia led me astray.

My godmother Doris described her friend Ruth Dross as a powerhouse, a gifted and independent woman who had made the most of every opportunity in life after being forced to flee Hitler's Germany.

Having left all her possessions behind, Ruth arrived alone in America in the guise of a tutor, a post concocted by a friend to get her out of Germany.

While Ruth carved out a wonderful new life for herself, she never forgot her homeland and whenever she could, bought and wore clothes and accessories made or designed in Germany. She found these glitzy German-made silver lamé shoes at a garage sale. They had never been worn and the heels were high enough to make the diminutive Ruth feel tall and a little like a movie star whenever she wore them.

When her eightieth birthday came along, she called Doris and Howard to ask if she could celebrate by visiting them at their favourite camping spot on Canandaigua Lake in New York State's Finger Lakes.

As a thank-you, Ruth gave Doris her beautiful silver shoes, the only things she felt she owned that were elegant enough for Doris's collection.

Sir Edward William Stafford served as Premier of New Zealand no less than three times between 1861 and 1872. He was also my great-great-grandfather.

Born to a life of privilege on the 23rd of April, 1819, Edward was the son of Berkeley Buckingham Stafford, of County Louth, Ireland. As a young man Edward yearned for adventure and abandoned his studies at Dublin's Trinity College to seek his fame and fortune in the wilds of New Zealand.

Settling in Nelson on the South Island in 1843, with his relatives the Tytlers he took up land for sheep farming and became involved in local politics. On the first of many trips to Australia, he brought back twelve hundred Merino ewes and Southdown rams, farming equipment and horses, along with bees and turkeys, the first ever to arrive in Nelson.

In 1853, he became the first Superintendent of Nelson Province. Among his many achievements throughout his long career, Edward was a proud ambassador for Nelson's wool on his regular trips to England.

This plaid wool crinoline might have been spun from Sir Edward's flock and worn on a chilly autumn day by one of his three daughters as she tended to orphaned lambs with her mother, Mary.

When my Granny Smith went to visit her grandmother Grace in 1919, it was an epic journey from Marblehead, a quaint seaside town on the coast of Massachusetts, to Brookline in Boston.

But she loved the adventure and getting dressed up in her favourite yellow dress almost as much.

One Sunday a month she would help her mother, Ethel, load up fresh fish and vegetables into Mr Eustis's carriage, which Granny adored riding in even if it did smell of manure. Formerly a funeral carriage, the cab was enclosed with black curtains and Granny liked to imagine that she was riding in Cinderella's golden coach.

Mr Eustis himself was fond of telling a good story and nothing could stop him once he started. If he was still going when they arrived home, he would simply pull up the horse at their front door and place a stone against the carriage wheel to stop it from rolling down the hill until he had finished his tale.

No doubt he thought Granny was a wonderful listener, but she was probably worlds away, dancing at the ball with her fairytale prince.

In 1895 Antoinette Fauchon lived just across the Seine from Le Bon Marché, the grandest department store in Paris.

As Antoinette was good friends with the Boileau family who owned it, they kindly tipped her off when a bolt of especially exquisite silk arrived in the store. Bearing the distinctive store label, this outfit was made from the finest black and cream striped silk she had ever seen.

A decade earlier when Émile Zola had used Le Bon Marché as the model for the department store in his *Au Bonheur des Dames (The Ladies' Paradise)*, Antoinette had feared the book would make her beloved store so popular it wouldn't need to sell beautiful silks any more.

But the true spirit of Le Bon Marché endured and it still stocked the best silks in France - and remained a ladies' paradise.

Woven into the stories behind the dresses my godmother collected over a lifetime are wonderful portraits of Doris and her many friends - strong, supportive and giving.

One such friend, Mithi Kirpalani, called Doris her American sister. In their later years, they would get together every month and spend hours looking through old photos and memorabilia.

Born in India, Mithi had met her husband when they were both studying at Oxford. When her husband joined the British diplomatic service, his postings took them all over the world. This 1960s evening gown, embroidered with metallic gold thread, was just one of the many elegant outfits Mithi wore to embassy events.

But Mithi was as renowned for her generosity to her friends as she was for her glamorous wardrobe. When she discovered Doris loved opals, she wrote to her sister in India asking her to find her an opal ring. Doris was over the moon when she received her precious gift. But sadly it was stolen when their house was burgled.

Mithi simply wrote to her sister again and had an even more beautiful opal ring delivered in time as a surprise for Doris and Howard's 50th wedding anniversary.

P erky Lloyd was pretty, petite and ... well, perky. Her favourite season was spring, a delightful time of year in the Dorset countryside where she lived. She loved to wander down the peaceful lanes gathering bluebells with her faithful whippets by her side.

Like all ladies of good sense and style in the 1820s, Perky was always sure to wear a bonnet outdoors to protect her porcelain skin from the ravages of the sun.

This was her best bonnet, woven by a Norfolk milliner from Leghorn straw, famous for its lightness and durability as well as its pale colour.

Perky chose the bonnet's silk lining herself to match her favourite dress and complement her peaches and cream complexion.

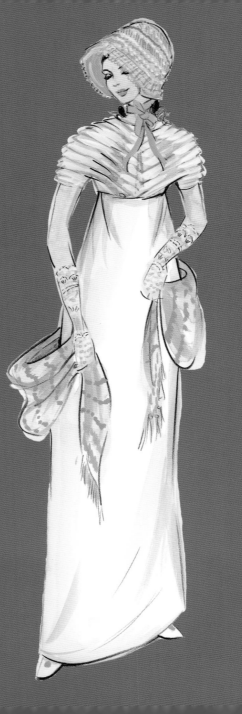

This exquisitely detailed 1915 lace gown given to Doris's mother, Faith, by a Quaker friend is a little piece of history.

Lucy had always been a woman Faith looked up to. Faith remembered her as outspoken, particular, capable and deeply involved in issues important to the Society of Friends, at home and abroad.

This dress represented an important turning point in Lucy's life because she wore it to an historic gathering of women at the Hague Conference in 1915. The Congress of Women called together hundreds of American and European women from twelve countries to try to stop the slaughter of the First World War.

Many of their initiatives were later embodied in President Wilson's Fourteen Points and led to the formation of the Women's International League for Peace and Freedom in 1919.

Little wonder that Lucy told Faith her dress was so precious that she must never, ever give it away to anyone who wouldn't appreciate it. When Faith passed it on to Doris she had to make the same promise. As have I.

Her story is an inspiring reminder of the extraordinary things women can achieve together.

'It's time we went to the Green Room. Will you come and pick me up? I'll make the reservation and pick up the tab.'

Edith Dewees would ring Howard and Doris to make this welcome announcement once a year, every year. As they lived on a tight budget, this excursion to the Hotel Dupont in Wilmington, Delaware, was a wonderful treat for them both.

Doris fondly remembers the buffets at the Green Room being so magnificent she didn't know where to begin so she always started with dessert, a strategy any sensible woman would understand. After piling her plate with mouth-watering cupcakes, trifles, custards and petit fours, she would move on to shrimp or roast beef.

Always impeccably dressed in outfits like this Norman Hartnell green plaid chiffon, Edith loved playing Lady Bountiful for her many friends, and they loved her for it.

For years after Edith passed away, they gathered at the Green Room for an annual 'Edith Dewees Memorial Dinner' in honour of their generous friend.

Francis Taplan sought out the best designer in Ohio to create this divine 1920s cream lace and turquoise silk dress to wear to her daughter's 10th wedding anniversary.

Francis chose Mikel Jerski of Cleveland because the designer managed to combine her three favourite features for a dress: fine lawn, delicate hand-worked lace and the finest silk. She also loved that he always left a signature of sorts somewhere on his dresses, a cluster of beaded flowers.

When Francis wore this dress to the anniversary party, the sinuous skirt and matching long scarf swirled around her as she danced, and she looked and felt absolutely splendid.

Sadly, three months later Francis died. Her daughter Emily could never bear to part with the dress because it reminded her how beautiful and happy her mother had looked that day.

It was not until she met Doris some fifty years later that she knew she had found the ideal custodian for her mother's very special dress.

Any night at the Metropolitan Opera is a glittering event, both on and off the stage, but a performance by the legendary Enrico Caruso presented New York's high society ladies with a solid gold opportunity to parade their most elaborate new ensembles.

On the night of Caruso's triumphant 1903 debut at the Met, the fashion stakes could not have been higher. Everyone who was anyone was there to hear the great Italian tenor sing in what promised to be the opera season's most lavish production yet: *Rigoletto*.

In the audience, Elizabeth Hosking watched on from one of the best seats in the house - a coveted private box bestowed on her family, thanks to her grandfather's efforts in helping to build the opera house twenty years earlier.

From her prime position above the crowd, Elizabeth knew that she would be on show, and in this spectacular embroidered wool opera coat, just arrived from Paris, her performance was pitch perfect.

Every girl in Toowoomba and Sydney in the 1940s and 1950s knew there was only one dressmaker to go to if you wanted an unforgettable wedding dress.

Ivy Spooner was revered by all brides-to-be for her fairytale creations of silk, satin, lace and tulle.

When one very special customer came to her with a drawing of her dream wedding dress, she knew this had to be the best one yet. Her niece Annette deserved nothing less.

Ivy tracked down the whitest of white lace from J.A. Grieg's 'The Silk Salon' in Sydney and worked night and day painstakingly sewing hundreds of pearls and sequins into the skirt and bodice of a superbly sculpted gown that flowed sinuously over layers and layers of tulle. She was quietly pleased the dress needed eight yards of lace, six yards of taffeta, eleven yards of tulle and ten yards of net.

Her niece looked like a princess - the most beautiful bride she had ever seen.

And twenty-six years later her great niece Alison looked just as radiant when she wore the same spectacular dress down the aisle.

Whenever Ethel Gilmore wore this sensational 1950s Ceil Chapman dress, with its brown mink fur collar and matching mink pill box hat, she felt a little like a film star.

Little wonder as the creator of this coffee cream silk brocade outfit was reputedly adored by Hollywood actresses from Marilyn Monroe to Elizabeth Taylor for the highly engineered fit of her fabulous gowns.

Always the perfect hostess, Ethel not only dressed the part but clearly loved opening her home to friends and giving back to the community. The second wife of one of Howard's friends and favourite colleague, Wheeler Gilmore, Ethel found a good friend in Doris.

Doris always said Wheeler could not have found a more loving wife and that they were role models for a perfect marriage. That they were clearly best friends as well as husband and wife also made them a pleasure to know.

Rebecca Edwards was just eighteen when she met the man she knew she wanted to spend the rest of her life with. It was the 1930s and Thomas Shannon had been sent straight from graduating at Princeton Theological Seminary to Rebecca's home town in West Virginia as a trial minister for her parish.

After two years it was clear not only to Rebecca, but everyone else in town that she and Thomas were meant for each other. However, young Thomas thought it inappropriate for a minister to fall in love with a member of the congregation so he tendered his resignation.

The small town rose up and Thomas's devoted congregation wrote letters protesting his resignation and begging him to stay on. Thomas relented and, after marrying his beloved Rebecca, served as minister for the next ten years. He always claimed that his decision to accept the 'call' to her town was God's way of introducing him to Rebecca.

And of course Rebecca was the model minister's wife, working tirelessly alongside her husband. Her coffee-coloured lace going-away outfit was a favourite at the more formal parish events because it reminded everyone of a love match the whole town had played a part in.

When one has one's own box at the Opera House in Paris, one must look the part. In 1900, Sarah Longfellow certainly knew how to do that and ensure that all eyes turned to her when she arrived with an elegant flourish of fine silk and feathers just before the curtain went up.

A devotee of the latest couture gowns by Jeanne Paquin, Sarah's hats were made by the best milliners on rue Montparnasse, and when she went to the opera she always carried an ostrich feather fan in one of her gloved hands.

Along with her ability to make an unforgettable entrance, Sarah was renowned for her collection of these feather fans, each more lavish than the other, commissioned from an exclusive boutique on rue de la Paix just two doors up from the House of Paquin.

It was said that her fellow opera goers often found watching Sarah more entertaining than what was happening on stage.

Having lived through three centuries, my English grandmother, May Stafford, had more than her fair share of Christmas mornings.

One of her favourite memories as a little girl was receiving this decadent purple silk velvet bodice with very grown-up jangly glass bead fringing and a matching skirt as a present.

It was 1899 and she was living with her wealthy aunt and uncle in Berkeley Square in London.

Part of their Christmas tradition was inviting the servants upstairs to the drawing room to receive their present. A large floppy parcel wrapped in brown paper was placed in each servant's arms, and with a quick bob or curtsey they would gratefully take their leave.

Much to her horror, Granny later found out that their 'present' was several yards of fabric to make next year's uniform. While it was explained that this was actually quite generous as in many households the servants had to pay for their own uniforms, Granny remained unconvinced.

So, when no one was looking she would sneak downstairs and leave her Christmas oranges and nuts on the servants' table.